On Being the Spark

On Being the Spark

Teachings from a Mystic Grandmother to her Granddaughter

Destiny McCune

On Being the Spark
Teachings from a Mystic
Grandmother to her Granddaughter
By
Destiny McCune

Published in 2021
Copyright © 2021 by Destiny McCune

Published by
DESTINY MCCUNE
2140 S ENSENADA CIR SE
RIO RANCHO, NM 87124

Some names have been changed to protect their privacy.

LIBRARY OF CONGRESS CATALOGING-IN-PUBLICATION DATA:
    Library of Congress Control Number: 2021915753

Printed in the United States of America
ISBN-13 978-1-7379174-0-3

~ She is art ~

CONTENTS

PART THREE
THE SPARK IN EARTHLY EVOLUTION

INTRODUCTION

I began the writing of this book with the intention of giving you, Angelina, as much of my knowledge as possible to help you to know yourself and the universe around you, to give you a head start, which would supply you with the tools to help you to make your way through life and hopefully a little more easily. These tools will not remove life's trials, the experiences that are destined for you, but they will help you to know how to respond to them, how to live through them gracefully, as love, in your full power and knowing of all that you are as a Spark of All-That-Is.

My desire was strong to teach you what I was able to teach my son, your Uncle Adam, and my daughter, your mother, Cristi, as we grew together over the years when it was just the three of us making our way in the world.

In my heart I know that you, the soul that you are in this lifetime as Angelina, were originally meant to be "born" into and as a child of mine, but circumstances, brought about by some of my previous life choices, changed that plan. That change set a new plan into motion, a backup plan. By mutual agreement of all parties involved (discussed on the higher, inner planes), you came into this particular existence of time and space through my daughter instead.

I had the privilege of providing two beautiful souls the opportunity to begin a new physical existence on this Earth as my children. Though I did not have the same opportunity with you, I was there at your birth to excitedly welcome you into the world.

As I stood at the side of the hospital bed where you and your mother were working hard to prepare for your entry, with the doctor in position to guide you gently into the world and seeing that your head was just beginning to emerge, she looked at me and said, "Would you like to touch her head?"

Surprised by the question and a bit apprehensive at first, wondering how your mom would feel about what I thought might be an intrusion into her and your miracle moments as mother and daughter, I moved myself close enough to see the matted, dark hair that covered the top of your glistening head. A quick glance at your mom let me know that she was fine with my being hands-on, or fingers-on as it were, in this part of the sacred ceremony of your birth, so I reached over with my left hand and lightly touched my fingertips to your crown chakra, the "soft spot" where you as soul enter and exit your body.

Only now do I realize how I truly participated in your birth process through my touch to your head. I do not recall connecting with you in words as thoughts in those few seconds, but I did connect spiritually. As a healer, I work with energy/light/love through the use of my intention for the good of the whole, allowing it to flow through me to be received by all that would accept the offer of it. Through my touch I facilitated your anointing, the blessing from All-That-Is for your sacred journey into this new life. A privilege, indeed.

As with every birth, when you emerged from the warmth of your mother's womb you were energetically imprinted with a sacred time/space energy "stamp" of the solar system as it was aligned and positioned at that moment. This astrological moment gave you many of your personality and behavioral influences that would more easily enable you to fulfill your soul's plan of all of the things that it (you) wanted to experience as Angelina. For that reason, you, and those who helped you to decide what your plan would entail, *chose* the moment of your birth.

You were born onto the planet of Earth in this lifetime as a soul with a plan, but also as a human with the power to choose your thoughts and how you will feel about what you perceive, in addition to how you will act, where you will go, what you will do—all of which can influence or change that soul plan. Hence, the answer to the question of whether life is destined or if it is made up of random choices is that it is both. You will find that the answer to many either/or type of questions is: *All of the above.*

Within me I feel the deep connection of our two souls, which compels me to fulfill my soul's contract with yours as I would have as your mother. Though as your grandmother, without the constant togetherness of living as mother and daughter wherein the teaching of life lessons flows naturally as we live out our experiences, there have been few opportunities to share with you the perspectives that I hold regarding the seen and the unseen worlds, what it means to be human and to give you reasons for and ways to navigate through your life to allow you to be all that you are as the love/light that you are as soul.

This book is a compilation of some of my own learnings, my wisdom gained, and my rememberings of truths that returned to me after being triggered by events in my own life, observations of others' lives and studies of a wide variety of writings over many years.

I originally began a recordkeeping of my stories and the teachings contained within them after your mother and Uncle Adam were born, with only them in mind as the recipients. So when it came to compiling the years of writings, I was not sure where to begin. I felt the weight of the task, wanting to make it perfect and perfectly understandable to you. How does one organize a lifetime of information, the stories that go along with them and the wisdom acquired as the result of having lived them?

Unable to answer that question for myself, I would begin the project and then stop, begin and then stop. Hence, for many years it remained merely an idea that left me feeling a growing pressure to produce tangibly into form as time passed.

What is the impetus that finally got me started in fulfilling this part of my soul's contract with you, Angelina? I had been receiving messages from Spirit, signs from the universe that it was time—actually past time I felt—to continue writing and putting together all of these writings, so on January 1, 2018, I decided that since it was a new year, it was the perfect time and that I would write something, anything, even just a sentence each day of the year in order to get started. But I realized that first I needed to let go of what had been holding me back from following through every other time--my desire for wanting perfection and for wanting to know what the final product would be and how it would read. I would need instead to just write whatever came to me, in whatever order it came to me, in the words in which it came to me, and the editing and rearrangement would come after. I needed to get out of my own way. And so it was.

The following is the outcome of those days spent compiling and writing my perceptions of the experiences of some of my life, the learnings, the rememberings of the ancient wisdom that is stored within my DNA that reawakened within me over time, such wisdom that I had acquired from my many existences/lives/experiences as a soul, as consciousness traversing the universes, the worlds of God/All-That-Is, before entering this life as Destiny.

To borrow a phrase from one of my favorite movies, this is my version of the truth, because it is from my perspective. As All-That-Is, or God, is ever expanding in its knowing of itself, so too is my knowing of the truth of it.

LETTER TO ANGELINA

My sweet Angelina, within these pages I have recounted for you events from my life as I experienced them along with the resulting information and wisdom that I gained from the perception and living of them. My experiences taught me about me. They taught me about life as a sentient being on this planet Earth and beyond. They reminded me of the reality that to be human is to be a soul, that Spark of Light that is the essence of Source/Creator/God/All-That-Is that is partially existing within and animating our physical bodies in order to experience from that Earthly human vantage point.

My experiences taught me and reminded me of all of these things, because I did not just live these events and then forget them. I observed them happening, and even later in time I analyzed and sought to ascertain their meanings, not just from a human level but also from what I call a spiritual level or nonphysical level once I became aware of or remembered that we are soul.

One of my spiritual teachers once called me a Quantum Physics Mechanic. Over time I have come to understand that phrase to mean that I have an ability to understand a part of how the physical reality and spiritual reality work together as one. In my mind, the way it works for me is that I am always seeing the two as one whole picture, and I am unable to think about them as separate when observing and analyzing the physical world.

When I see an event in our physical reality, I can instantly know some of the spiritual laws working within that event and, therefore, why that event is unfolding the way that it is. For that reason, I am also good at understanding people—who they are inside and their underlying beliefs about themselves, broadly speaking, and the spiritual laws at work in their lives based on those beliefs. I am helped also through my ability to feel their energies.

It is my wish that as you read about my life and my view of life that you find a deeper meaning, clarity and understanding of your own life, far beyond what you have come to know already through our times together thus far.

These are my stories, my vision of the world and beyond as I have come to know and remember them through the living of my life as Destiny.

I love you dearly,
Grandma

PART ONE

BEING
THE SPARK

1

ALL-THAT-IS –
THE TRUTH OF YOUR BEING

Self-love is essential and is generally what most people lack. Why is self-love essential? And essential to what? Self-love is essential to the ability to perceive yourself and the world as they are in truth, through the lens of the all-inclusiveness of that love. The untruths are unmasked through this internal self-awareness, and all is observed through this unwavering knowing of who you are as a light of All-That-Is.

Self-love is essential in order to keep yourself from believing in the untruth that your experiences will often seem to be telling you, which is that you are less than a beautiful Spark of All-That-Is, and as such, you are undeserving, unworthy, unlovable.

Self-love is essential to maintaining your internal wisdom while navigating in this world of form, your life here on Earth. As the basis, the foundation around which your perceptions become internalized, your realizations are able to be made from this foundation of love of self. With a stable foundation of self-love securely set within, each outside experience can only be perceived from this basis.

It is the harshness of this world of polarity, that creates the trials that can harden your heart to yourself and others. Existing in the harsh environment of the Earth serves the purpose of expanding awareness through the experience of opposites. Or, I should say, that that is your purpose for being here on Earth instead of some other form of existence of All-That-Is. You come here as soul manifested within a human body in order to experience one of the greatest learning places—greatest because of its extreme challenges and, therefore, containing more possibilities through those experiences to remember who you are as soul, a Spark of All-That-Is.

All-That-Is has been referred to by many names, and probably the most familiar would be God. Some envision God with a body I believe because it is easier to contemplate a loving, powerful essence in a form, one with which they can identify. Infinite, all encompassing light/love consciousness is intangible and, therefore, harder to comprehend as a human being.

It is not until one's consciousness as soul in human form is no longer identifying itself as being only a human and, therefore, no longer thinking of itself as separate from All-That-Is, that it is able to remember that it is one with it, it is it, and it has never been anything else.

In human form it has been playing a game of being the manifestation of the light and love of All-That-Is that is hidden from itself and others behind the belief of an illusory reality.

The truth is that each Spark of All-That-Is is of the same

essence. When you, as this essence, are born onto this Earth plane existence, you begin to identify yourself through what you experience here as an individual and forget your true essence of oneness with, and of, All-That-Is—which is the point of being here in the first place, to remember what you are.

All-That-Is knows that it exists, but only in manifestation could All-That-Is experience itself. So it created the many denser worlds of form with which to experience itself in form. All-That-Is sent out parts of itself, sparks of light, consciousness, souls that are us, into these worlds of form to experience itself. Earth is one of these worlds, but there are many.

All-That-Is vibrates at the speed of love, which is the fastest rate of vibration, and you are a Spark of All-That-Is, hence you, the soul that you are, vibrates at the speed of love as well. In addition to coming into a life on Earth in order to experience for All-That-Is as that spark, through identifying with yourself as an individual human in this life, as well as all that you have learned over all of your lives, you have come to continue to grow in awareness of your true soul self and to embody that true self more. In other words, you have come to *be* the love that you are as soul through your body, living as the light of love.

The vibration of light/love affects everything around it of lower vibration by energetically lifting it into higher vibration, so essentially into more light and love. This is a spiritual law. By being the love that you are in all that you do and think and feel, you are changing and lifting into light not only your life, but the lives of those around you and the world.

The challenge for your life is growing into holding and embodying more of the light of love that you already are. The goal is to be love in action.

2

EVERYTHING VIBRATES

Beyond time and space of the lower worlds of All-That-Is are the higher vibrating realms or what can be thought of as the spiritual realms, because soul exists as spirit there without dense physical bodies. They can also be thought of as higher dimensions. Everything everywhere vibrates at different rates, which is what gives it its particular form or energetic.

Each realm vibrates at different rates, the lower, denser, physical, material areas vibrating the slowest, and then the closer you get to All-That-Is, the faster it vibrates. These faster vibrating areas cannot be experienced by you in and through the physical form from the denser areas, because you are vibrating too slowly to be in resonance with them.

Think of it as how you experience water in its various forms of vibration. Water vibrating very slowly is dense and becomes ice. As ice melts and becomes water, it is vibrating faster than solid ice. When water vibrates even faster than its state of being water, it becomes vapor.

Notice that all of these rates of vibration exist in the same space simultaneously. Though you do not usually see the higher worlds of Spirit with your physical eyesight, because you are vibrating too slowly to do so, they exist in the same space in which you exist.

As an example, imagine that as you go about your day, perhaps walking through your house, you could be moving through the energy of a spirit guide or a loved one who is in the spirit realm now, or even when you are in nature you might be sharing the same space with a fairy or nature spirit as you walk through its energy because it is invisible to you from your slower vibrating vantage point.

3

SOUL FAMILY

Each soul will have numerous incarnations, spirit into flesh as a human, as well as spirit in various vibratory incarnations of light in various dimensions and universes. Just as you have a human biological family and additionally you belong to the larger group of the human family, you also have soul families that have existed since your creation. The emergence of these families began at the beginning when God created the monad, which created the soul, which created the soul extensions.

The best, most succinct, description of the creation of the sparks of light that we are, and I believe the easiest to understand of all the explanations that I have come across, was written by Joshua David Stone in his book titled *The Complete Ascension Manual: How to Achieve Ascension in this Lifetime.* He wrote:

"In the beginning God created sons and daughters

in the spiritual state. He created what are esoterically called 'monads' or individualized spiritual sparks of the Creator. It is the monad that has also been called the 'I Am Presence.' That was our first core intelligence and our first individualized identity.

"This divine spark, also called spirit, is our true identity. The monad, or spiritual spark, decided with its free choice that it wanted to experience a denser form of the material universe than it was living in.

"Each of our monads, with the power of its mind, created twelve souls. It is as though the monad puts down twelve fingers of fire, and at the end of each finger are the twelve individualized souls. Each soul is a smaller and partial representation of its creator, the monad. The soul has also been referred to as the higher self, the superconscious mind, and the higher mind.

"What we have here so far is that God created infinite numbers of monads, or spiritual sparks, and each monad then created twelve souls to experience a denser form of matter than previously experienced. Each soul, then desiring to experience an even denser form of the material universe, created twelve personalities or soul extensions who incarnated into the densest material universe. We on Earth are personalities, or soul extensions, of our soul, just as our soul is an extension of a greater consciousness which is our monad. Our monad is an extension of an even greater consciousness which is God, the Godhead, the Father and Mother of all creation.

"So each of us on Earth has a soul family, so to speak, of eleven other soul extensions. The eleven other soul extensions could be incarnated on the Earth or on

*some other planet in God's infinite universe. Our
other soul extensions could also not be incarnate in a
physical body at this time but could be existing on one
of the other spiritual planes of existence.*

*"Our eleven other soul extensions or personalities
could be looked at as our immediate soul family. Ex-
tending this metaphor further, we also then have an
extended monadic family. Each of us has twelve in
our soul group and one hundred forty-four in our
monadic group."*

Some soul family members will typically incarnate together in the same time and space for interaction with each
other and to assist in each others' learnings and experiences. As soul family, we come together again and again in
different forms, different lives in different times, different
space, different planets, different dimensions.

In the early 2000s I began researching our family's geneal-
ogy and compiling the information into an ancestral chart
that includes many census records, documents and photographs. While compiling this information, one day I realized that since as a soul family we usually incarnate together
over and over again, then our family line on Earth would
consist of these same souls returning to play a different part
with the same soul family group of humans, which means
that in many cases we are our ancestors.

In my genealogical research I began to notice that several of the birth dates or death dates (month and day only,
of course) from the past coincided with other family members' birth dates or death dates of a more recent time.
Partly because I know that nothing in creation is acciden-

tal or coincidental, and mostly because I feel the truth of it inside of me, and knowing that there is astrological significance to the individual birth times and dates that our souls are stamped with, I believe that those lives that share the same birth and/or death month and day were, at least in some cases, lived by the same soul.

I came across such an occurrence of matching dates when I discovered that the death day of my great, great grandfather is the same as my day of birth. That information, combined with the familiarity I felt towards him after delving into his life story, has convinced me that I, as a piece of my greater soul family, was my great, great grandfather.

Often we are our ancestors reincarnating into new life experiences together in the same time frame to resolve life issues that were left unresolved from those lifetimes. How are issues left unresolved and what are they? Unresolved issues can be thought of as energy imbalances brought about by misperceptions and fears that were carried with the soul as it transitioned out of the body that it left upon what is referred to as death. These unresolved issues create an energetic stamp on the soul that can be referred to as a karmic imprint that needs to be brought into balance through love in a subsequent life experience, often with the same soul with whom the imbalance was created.

There is a continuity of life experience after life experience that is a continual expansion of soul knowing itself, remembering itself while being in form, whether human or otherwise.

4

THE BEGINNING

You begin all of your Earthly journeys first in the spirit world as soul gathering with those higher beings who will help you to choose what to experience in your life and what personality traits and issues to bring forward in your life, some in order to resolve and balance them energetically through the experience of them. You make a plan for each life that can include directions that you want to take in career, lifestyle, life circumstances and specific people that you want to meet. All of these factors enable you to fulfill your chosen life purpose and obtain the learnings, rememberings and karmic energy balances that you wish to attain.

Your higher soul self and your individual guides help to keep you on that chosen life path by whispering in your etheric inner ear suggested choices to make when it is essential to your staying on your path. It is up to you to develop an ability to hear or feel the nudges that you receive from them by taking time regularly to quiet your mind and go within yourself. This exercise of stilling the mind is often thought of as meditation.

Meditation is a way of centering yourself within your soul self where you focus on nothing outside of you, where your consciousness can expand into the quiet, peaceful nothingness and everythingness of All-That-Is. In this space where you are just being, communication from your higher soul self that mostly exists outside of your human body (its frequency being too high for it to exist totally within your body), is able to be felt and heard by you more easily.

You will recognize your higher soul self's guidance and communication as intuition, knowings and feelings of what choices are appropriate for you to make as you go about your life. There is no reasoning from your mind involved in this communication. It will be a sense of knowing without reason what step to take next on your path as circumstances are presented to you in the moment.

A question that is often asked is, *Are our lives destined or do we have a choice?* My answer is that it is not a question of either/or—it is both. You have your destined path, that which was chosen before your birth into your life, but you also have free will to make your choices as situations present themselves to you. Some of these choices may take you off of your path, but your higher self and guides are constantly working behind the scenes in the unseen realms to try to guide you gently back to fulfill your soul's plan.

There are key people that you plan to meet in each life who are scheduled to "arrive" at a particular time who will play pivotal roles in your life. As souls, these people have generously agreed to play a part in your life experience in order that you may receive the gift of learning or karmic balancing that you desired before coming into this life. They, too, are receiving the same gift from you.

These people will play various parts in your life experience. Some will be love relationships, some will be special friendships, some family members, each with their own role to play of providing what you need in order to experience a chosen life theme or themes. Some will come to you to play the part of antagonist, those who will bring the opposite of love to your life, for instance, that will result in an experience of pain, disappointment, sadness, anger.

These antagonists can be experienced on an individual level or be perceived on a global level. They all affect your life to whatever degree you allow them to influence your feelings about yourself. The key is to not allow them to influence how you see or know yourself to be as a beautiful being of light.

Remember that these antagonists have chosen out of love for you as soul to play this part for your own growth and learning. When you can know and feel that truth within, then you will know that truly there is nothing to forgive.

Sometimes, for instance, a soul will wish to know and explore the feeling of empathy during its life in human form, so it will need to be in a situation that allows for it to empathize with another being, or perhaps the opposite where others are empathizing with it. The same is true for all feelings and topics that a soul might want to experience in each lifetime.

In this way, it can be seen that there is no right or wrong in a soul's chosen path, so no judgment should be made. No one can know what another person's soul plan is and, therefore, cannot know its chosen learnings for its lifetime.

Strive in life to look at life through the eyes of your Divine Self, your soul, through the eyes of love and compassion, observing but not judging, unattached to the outcome not only of your situations, but especially to those of others. When you perceive everything through the eyes of truth, that is, through the higher consciousness of your soul, and acknowledge all as being that same truth of the light of All-That-Is, you are lifting all that you perceive through that acknowledgment into resonance with its own Divine Self.

5

KNOW THYSELF

No one but you can know what's in your mind and heart, and it is not your business what others think or say about you, negative or positive. Their minds and thoughts, their feelings and lives are their business and their own to work through and live.

If you allow yourself to be influenced by others' negative thoughts about you, where you let yourself feel less than you are or not enough as you are, then you are not acknowledging and loving yourself as the Spark of All-That-Is. Because of their own insecurities, there will always be those who will want to make themselves feel better about themselves by making you feel bad about yourself. When you are able to recognize that this is the dynamic that is occurring, it is easier to turn your focus from your hurt to compassion for the misperceptions and low self-esteem that they have about and for themselves and the lack of self-love that they feel within.

Insecurities are a part of everyone's life as a human, to lesser or greater degrees, and are some of the many beliefs about yourself that can cause you to feel inadequate or not enough, and which in turn can hinder your confidence to live the life that you want to live and be who you want to be. Often insecurities begin when you believe the untruths that others tell you about yourself.

Insecurities are transformed first through their acknowledgment and then through the introspective process of digging down to the root cause, the root belief or misperception that you hold about yourself that has caused you to feel the way that you do about yourself. Once you are able to expose the underlying belief, you are able to change it. Beliefs can be changed. It is just a belief—it is not the truth about you. The truth of you is that you are the beauty, light and love of soul and all that that encompasses.

Diminishing your light for another or because of another in order to influence their thoughts about you or to try to make them feel better about themselves is a popular lesson in self-love that humans choose to learn. It is never appropriate or beneficial to you, your life, or others around you to purposely lower your frequency for any reason. It is an action chosen out of fear, not love.

Instead, by being and shining your light, you automatically lift the frequency all around you that will enable others the opportunity to resonate with their higher octaves and thereby shift into their light. Remember yourself as this light, and stay true to yourself always.

It is easy to let the fear of loneliness or the fear of not being accepted to sway you to choose someone to be your friend who is not truly your friend, because their heart is not open to you, and this person does not treat you and acknowledge you as a friend would—with kindness and support and appreciation for who you are. Then, in order to keep this person in your life, you allow yourself to be treated poorly.

You lose your brightness, your light becomes dimmed as you begin to believe that you do not deserve better for yourself, that you will not have any friends if you do not hold onto this association no matter how negative you feel about yourself as a result. You begin to believe the illusion of the experience instead of the truth of who you are and what you are.

What truly matters in every experience is your response to it. It will show you who you are being, and it will create what you will attract to you in your life. You always have a choice in how you will respond.

When you choose to be in a situation that causes your light to dim, you are acknowledging to the universe that you do not love yourself, and you will energetically draw to you more experiences wherein you are not being loved until you can finally love yourself.

Though no one wishes to be alone all of the time, once you truly love yourself, human flaws and all, those times when you are by yourself, appreciating yourself and being grateful for your life, you will feel the contentment of being in your own company, alone but not lonely.

6

OBSERVATION
OR JUDGMENT

It is not appropriate to judge another person, because in doing so, you are not living through your higher soul. All-That-Is does not judge. When you are living through your higher soul, then you live and create your life from love instead of fear. You cannot know what the complete underlying truth of a situation is, and you do not know what that soul's chosen path is.

There is a difference between judgment and observation. When you observe, you notice what is happening from a point of neutrality, where you are not assigning from your point of view whether the event or person is good, bad or anything in between. Instead you are merely taking note of the facts as you perceive them.

It is not an easy thing to do to remain impartial or detached when coming to conclusions, because it is part of being human while living in this world of opposites to feel the need to pick a side. Remaining neutral without judgment, or being able to see all sides and from the higher perspective of your soul, will allow you to feel compassion for those involved in an event that brings hurt or struggle to them without losing your balance by going down into the lower frequency with them.

Throughout my life I have been hesitant to use the words *I am proud of you* to your mom and uncle. For an unknown reason that I did not explore then, it did not feel right for me to feel proud of someone else. Now I know the reason to be that my being proud of someone implies my approval of their choice, though their choice does not need my approval, because only they can know what is the right choice for them, the choice that will bring them the greatest joy or fulfillment in the moment.

Even when I empathized with their feeling of accomplishment, pride was not what I was feeling. I felt the joy of knowing that they were coming into their own sense of self through their accomplishments, and I was happy that they were happy.

By definition, my use of the word *proud* ultimately would imply a judgment on my part, that something someone did was what I deemed to be good. I, personally, might feel that what they did was a positive thing, but the truth is that no one can make that judgment about another's choice of path, because no one can know what the fulfillment of one's path should look like, where and how it should go and what needs to be experienced by that soul along the way.

I also did not want your mom and Uncle Adam to look outside of themselves for validation. I knew that it needed to come from within themselves individually to know their own sense of self worth.

As a human, it is nice to have validation from others, and I can see its usefulness as an individual stepping stone as you climb higher and more firmly into your own sense of self, self worth and confidence. Yet an overemphasis or need of outside validation can become a dependency that can keep you from relying on your own internal knowing by always looking outside of yourself.

In relying on others' opinions about you and your life, you are giving your power away to them, unconsciously allowing them a superior position over you and in your mind making their beliefs more credible than your own.

I believe each person needs a feeling of support from those closest to them—support without judgment—that will ultimately teach them how to think and feel independently, to build the knowing and confidence that they are capable and can trust themselves, through their perfectly imperfect human self, to maneuver through this life. Along the way they will discover that they are, and have, everything that they need within themselves.

Your greatest gift, as a Spark of All-That-Is, is the power to choose. Whatever you choose to do, do it for yourself, not because you want to receive the approval of another. The appreciation of those who are special to you is a nice-to-have, but is by no means necessary or important to your well being when you know that your true and lasting well being comes from how you think about yourself in the knowing of the spark that you are.

7

DISCERNMENT
OF ACTION

Allow your higher self to be your guide, knowing that all of your answers are within you. There is an expression in the world—let your conscience be your guide. Your higher self is your conscience, and it will guide you to know what is appropriate for you in your thoughts, in your feelings, in your actions, in the fulfillment of your life's purpose.

Know who you are and know that you are the light of All-That-Is and express yourself as that through your human attributes, talents, passions. Infuse love and light into all of your creations, all of your actions, all of your thoughts, all of your words. Be the love that you are, and you will lift and change the world around you to match that vibration.

Though I know that there is a reason for negative events, a learning experience for those involved, there are times when I have encountered a particular scene—such as two kids fighting on a playground, or a physical and verbal altercation between a man and a woman, or a sobbing four-year-old boy running after his mother's car as she drove away from him in order to teach him a lesson—whereby I feel compelled to intercede, to stop it, because it hurts me to see people hurting each other.

What did that mother who left her son teach him? She taught him the fear of abandonment.

In those instances I am confronted with the dilemma of deciding the right action. I do not fear for myself, so that is not part of the equation in making my choice. I trust and know that I am always protected. Sometimes I choose a verbal intervention, and I take action in that way because I forget that I can lift the energy with my intention, but most often the first thing that I will do is to call in the light of All-That-Is to surround and fill all involved in order to lift the frequency to that which is for the highest good of all. I will also call in a blue light for calmness and peacefulness. Then I wait to see the results.

Each time that I have shifted the frequency in that way, I have witnessed the effect of how it was felt by those who were surrounded by it, which was that it had allowed them to shift their own energies.

8

EXPLORATION
OF SELF

You have sometimes expressed your concern that you are not what you would call spiritual, because in your mind you believe that you do not have psychic abilities or feel or hear messages from your guides or see signs from Spirit. Let me reassure you that most people, including myself, were not born with these inner senses open. They developed and opened as I fine-tuned my mind and body through meditation and contemplation to lift in frequency, which allowed my higher self to lead the way, and they strengthened over time from my recognition, focus and use of them.

Eventually, through your own experience and curiosity, you will discover pieces of the spiritual puzzle and begin to see how they all fit together and how they make sense of and tie together the spiritual with the material world that you live in now.

This exploration of self is one of the reasons that I have come into this life as Destiny and then to share what I have learned with others—to help them remember who they are as All-That-Is and what it means to be that. Another reason that I am on Earth at this chosen time is to be here to participate in its and humanity's ascension into a higher vibrational dimension of time and space.

I was struck by the knowing of this truth early in my life when I spoke to a friend the words that emerged from my subconscious that, "I am not here for me; I am here for humanity." The acknowledgment of that statement was felt by me as a weight of responsibility, but at the same time a privilege to have the opportunity to be of service.

You, too, have decided to be here now to contribute to this shift into higher consciousness. Your contribution may be given in any way that you choose, but remember that all that is truly required is that you be the light and love that you are in expression.

As had happened with me, once you discover and know who you are and what it means to your life experience, that knowledge will change you with its realizations and forthcoming wisdom.

For one, you will know, and therefore feel, that there is truly nothing to fear. You lose your fear of the unknown, of the uncontrollable moments before you, when you realize and trust that all is in divine order and perfection always and that nothing can harm you, the real you, because you are eternal. In my view it is senseless to fear this life since it is all an illusion. It is just your soul playing a game by placing its focus in this particular time and space.

9

CREATING THE
ADVENTURE

All that you experience has a purpose, something that it is showing you about how you have been and/or are being. Your experience is the result of, and created by, the energy that you emanate and are therefore attracting to you as well as soul-chosen events, all of which allow you the opportunity to see yourself more clearly. The key to choosing the desired energetic circumstances that you will create and draw to you is to learn to respond through your heart-mind instead of reacting in fear-based actions that are outside of the vibration of love/light.

Life appears to be a continuous set of coincidental circumstances presenting themselves to you that you will need to react to, ready or not, whether you believe you are capable, and where you often fear that you are not. When you know that you are always capable and that there is always a solution to a problem, even if that solution is to do nothing in the moment, and that no matter what, you will be guided by those on the "other side" in the higher dimensions in order to keep you on your soul's path, even with the detours you may take through your own choices, then life becomes an exciting adventure where you can embrace change as it happens, because of all the newness that it will bring.

Through this knowing, you carry your feeling of safety within you no matter what you do, which allows you to travel through life's challenges confident that although you may be left briefly battered or bruised or thrown off balance, you can emerge unscathed.

I consider myself to be fearless, but in no way does that mean that I do not experience some form of fear as an immediate reaction to something, say perhaps a thought I might have or even being startled by an unknown and unexpected movement or noise or even the fear that comes from exposing myself in the writing of this book to all of the opinions, positive and negative, that will naturally come of it.

I do not want to be the center of attention in that way, yet I am driven through my nature as a teacher to communicate what is within me, to inspire others to know themselves and to be all that they are as soul. This has been another of my life's struggles—how to remain behind the scenes and yet not.

Perhaps I should have written this book a long time ago, before the creation and widespread use of opinion-laden social media outlets, when it was possible to remain under the radar. Now it's a little too late. Oh well…

All kidding aside, another part of me knows that this is my destiny and that I am always in the right time and the right place. This is where, once again, I put my knowing into action and actually live it. I know the ride will be bumpy, but I know that I will not only come out intact, but I will have experienced another grand adventure. And I do love a good adventure.

When you realize that what you believe to be true will be true *for you*, you will know that you hold the power to experience the kind of life that you wish through the beliefs that you hold true and by allowing your soul self to be your guide along your path. You will know that your point of power is your ability to choose what you will think and do and how you will feel in each moment of now, and that nothing can happen to you except in accordance with your consciousness, that which is the culmination of all of your experiences as soul and the frequency at which you vibrate.

When you know the laws of Spirit, in particular the Law of Attraction and Law of Cause and Effect (which is the Law of Karma), you will realize that because everything is of Source (All-That-Is) energy and that you are constantly using that energy to create your life, qualifying its love/light with your thoughts, feelings and actions, you will know that the energy that you qualify with the vibration of hatred, will be attracted back to you with the same vibration of hatred. You will experience that vibration of hatred in your own life. The same is true of any vibration including love, kindness, generosity.

So which will you choose? What do you want your life to vibrate as? What do you want to receive? It is always your choice.

The way of creative manifestation has always been the same as a human. You create through thought, feeling, knowing and belief, by imbuing the Divine Source light that you breathe into you with those qualities of vibration which then emanate out from you, drawing to you the resonating vibrations.

Earth and all of its inhabitants, are in the process of ascending, or in other words embodying more light of Divine Source and lifting in consciousness, which coincides with shifting into a faster rate of vibration. The magnetics are changing, allowing our thought/feeling creations to manifest more quickly than in the past. They can be seen in our lives more instantaneously.

Most of the life circumstances that we find ourselves in were created unconsciously, without intention, as our minds threw out our random thought/feeling vibrations. Whether consciously chosen or unconsciously manifesting, it all happens through the fulfillment of the Law of Cause and Effect.

10

RELEASING PAIN

You cannot change anyone. You can only change your-self. So when you can understand that you cannot expect others to be what and how you want them to be, because they can only be who they are capable of being in each moment, then you are able to forgive and let go of your ideas of how things should have been. And when you are able to forgive yourself for your expectations and forgive others for their actions, the only actions that they were capable of expressing in the moment, then you are released and no longer holding onto the pain that you felt.

Ultimately, through those and all experiences, negative or positive, you are to realize something about yourself. That is their purpose. The question to always ask yourself is, "What am I learning from this situation?" And if you are encoun-tering the same learning about yourself over and over again from similar situations that are not pleasant and that you would rather not be a part of, then it is time to start making different choices instead of the same ones over and over again that bring the same results. Choose actions that are in alignment with and a reflection of the love of yourself.

When contemplating how I think about my past experiences and their lack of effect upon me in the present, I realized that, unlike many, when I think about my past sad, disappointing or painful experiences, I do not still have those sad, disappointed or hurt emotions attached to them. I wondered what makes me different. What beliefs do I hold that allow me to perceive differently and therefore respond differently than many others?

The answer that I came to was that I am able to see the emotionally negative experiences that I lived through in a detached way, without judgment, remembering them without feeling them. I can remember that they were not happy times and that I experienced pain or disappointment, but I no longer feel the depth of pain that I felt while I was living them.

I liken it to childbirth—I remember, when thinking back on it, that it was extremely painful, but I cannot recall or re-experience the depth of the physical pain. It is just a memory, and the memory of the pain is never as painful as the actual experience.

Along the way I have processed each of these events within me to come to the realization that I had a part to play in them. Whether decided by my higher soul that my participation in an experience would be just what I needed, or whether I consciously or unconsciously made the choice to be a part of it, I have accepted responsibility for those choices. I cannot blame another for the circumstances in which I find myself based on my conscious choices nor through what I have blindly drawn to me that is in resonance with the frequency of the thoughts that I think and the emotions that I feel.

In all situations that I found myself a part of where I was interacting with someone who did not treat me well, I realized in my processing that every person does the best that they can with what they have to work with mentally and emotionally. Meaning that who they are at that time mentally and emotionally may not have been intelligently thoughtful and caring, but it was where they were developmentally in consciousness, and nothing more could be expected of them.

A person cannot be caring if their heart is not open, and therefore, one cannot expect that of them. A person cannot be considerate if they are only capable of thinking of their own self, and therefore, one cannot expect that of them. And on it goes. Unfortunately, though, knowing that truth does not make it any less irritating or hurtful in the moments that the painful events are happening.

11

THE FREQUENCY
OF LOVE

Life is filled with opportunities to make choices from love instead of from fear—love of self most importantly and firstly, and then love of others—the choices that you make out of love for yourself and then how you love others in the way that you choose to treat them or respond to them, even when they are being a version of their worst self. When you communicate from love, whether the words are in your head or spoken, your only desire in the moment is that love be expressed and felt in order to bring about the highest outcome for all.

Anger brings out your worst self that does not allow your words and actions to come from a place of love. Transmute the anger by recognizing it, feeling it, and then go within yourself to determine the true, core, deepest reason for your anger, preferably before you speak. Once you know what the core reason is, you will be able to think through logically, without emotion, and realize what you think about yourself, those misperceptions about yourself, or the fears that you believe in that have caused you to be angry. Then, from that new realization, you know a new truth that will automatically shift your emotions from anger to a more heart-based feeling.

The only real truth about yourself is that you are love, because you are a Spark of All-That-Is, and any other belief that you hold that is counter to that truth is false and, therefore, can be changed when you decide that that belief does not serve you and is no longer what you want to believe is true. This is how you change your beliefs—by seeing and understanding the falseness of what you thought to be true about yourself and/or your perception of life.

Once you change your thoughts, your emotions automatically change to coincide with them. Essentially your new, higher thoughts are enabling you to feel new, higher emotions, which coincides with an opening of your heart, allowing you to be the love/light that you are as a soul. Your anger will disappear because you now know rationally a deeper truth about a situation that is beyond your ego, that is outside of that small "I" self, because it encompasses the expanded view from a higher perspective, which is that of your larger soul self.

I will give you an example from my own experience of how this works.

I was analyzing a situation, a relationship that I had chosen to be in that did not turn out as I had desired and that I ended. In my mind it should have ended long before it did, but I realized that I could not release it until I had an understanding of it, and me in relation to it, though most of my conclusions and revelations would come after the ending of it.

After feeling my pain, the hurt from my perception of being callously and coldly treated, in my ensuing analysis of the experience while being detached from my emotion, I was able to come to understandings about the relationship and myself within the relationship. I could see who I was and who I did not want to be, which enabled me to be different.

From a higher perspective view, there is no judgment about whether a situation is good or bad—it is just information and realization—and from this place of no judgment, anger and blame dissipate and fade away, and what happens as a result is an opening of the heart.

Being the love that you are is the result, and you may find that from this place of love your one desire in the moment will be to let the person(s) involved know that all is well and that you wish them well. At least that is how it is for me.

Forgiveness is often a difficult state to achieve, yet it is essential for letting go of misperceptions, of old beliefs that do not serve you in your life, and allowing you to change and begin life anew as a new person. It can be achieved through the same intellectual, mindful introspection and opening of your heart that I previously described.

The surprising discovery that you will make, though, once you have reached a point in your heart of forgiveness, where you are perceiving the situation from your highest soul self, is that there was nothing, truly, to forgive.

Your personal perception, your view and experience of your life is different from all others' based on its unique perspective, which is the reason why when two people witness or participate in the same event in the same moment, they will perceive different things about the event and what happened in it. The event is seen through each individual's beliefs and biases. Each will see what they creatively drew to them that is in resonance with the energetic quality of the thoughts and feelings that they sent out from themselves that by spiritual law must return to them with a matching quality.

Once you realize that you hold a responsibility of being within an experience, either by way of being the cause through attracting or resonating with like or in-kind energies that you have sent out from yourself, thereby being in agreement with the experience, or that it was chosen or agreed to by your soul, then you must also realize logically that you cannot blame anyone for any of your circumstances. Hence, if you cannot blame anyone for your circumstances and experiences, then there is nothing to forgive.

Remember that not only did your soul agree to your having that experience, but every other person's soul self had chosen or had been in agreement with them having the experience with you. You were not in this alone.

At this point you might want to say, "Yes, but this person said or did terrible, hurtful things to me. How can I forgive them for that?"

In seeing the situation from the big picture of the higher soul's point of view, yes there is nothing to forgive, but, arguably, from the human perspective, people were mistreated through words or actions. Though the overall experience was chosen or agreed to on a soul level, on the human level there were choices made by each individual involved, whether consciously or unconsciously, in how they were going to act and what they were going to think and say in relation to the other(s). So from this human perspective there can be the need to forgive those others and yourself.

What I have come to understand, though, is that as a human we each individually are only capable of comprehending and perceiving (and therefore acting) from the level of our consciousness in each moment, what we believe to be true based on our experiences, and we are bound by and limited by that. Knowing this allows me to understand that everyone is doing the best that they can from their own level of consciousness, which in turn has allowed me to forgive the actions and intentions of others. Essentially, they know not what they do.

12

ARE YOU ACTING FROM LOVE OR FEAR?

An action that is chosen out of fear instead of love can be difficult to recognize when you are not aware that you even have the fear. The beliefs that you hold within as fears can be subtle influencers of your mind, but those beliefs can be brought to light by noticing your choices and then, through introspection, becoming aware of the reasons for your choices. Those reasons hold the answers to what fearful beliefs are within you.

For instance, how many people truly recognize when they are being manipulative? Wanting and trying to manipulate someone else or a situation can be the result of having a fear of not being in control, instead of trusting that the universe is providing you with all that you require. You are sending the signal to the universe that you do not believe that all of your needs are and will be met, and then the universe complies with that thought by producing and bringing to you the matching result, or resonance, of your belief—situations where you will perceive that you are lacking what you need in your life.

Additionally, the act of manipulation towards another person works against the laws of the universe in that you are attempting to interfere with someone's free will.

From my experience, when you are in flow with the universe, your life will flow smoothly—not without problems, but smoothly. Yet when you push against it in trying to make something happen outside of the flow, it either does not work or it does not last, and it falls apart. In other words, the universe does not support it. The universe supports all things of the vibration of love, unity and harmony.

Accepting a job that you do not want and that you will not be happy in for fear that if you do not take whatever job that you can get, you will not have money to survive, or allowing yourself to be in a relationship that you are unhappy in because you feel that you need help financially or that you are afraid to be alone are other examples of acting from fear.

The fears that you have are meant to be recognized and overcome in this life. Always choose from the love and appreciation of yourself and all, and you will be rewarded with more opportunities to receive love in all of its forms.

In order to continue to grow and evolve to be the best that you can be and live as the love that you are, introspection is essential. One question to always ask yourself after being in a situation that evoked negative reactions within you or others is: "Could I have done something differently or said something differently to make that situation better?"

Never mind about what the other person or people could

have done or said differently, even though they too most assuredly could have done or said things in another way to make the situation better. It is not your business to determine what others should think or say or how they should act. Your business is knowing yourself and deciding how *you* want to be in response to how they are being.

Being your best self, your loving self, will attract to your world more of the same love in all of its many forms through the spiritual Law of Attraction.

When answering that question of what you could have done differently, look at yourself, others and the situation honestly, without blame or judgment. Were you coming from a place of love within yourself when you spoke your words? Your words will always be more accepted and heard when love is behind them, when they are spoken with love and kindness, with the goal of wanting to be understood instead of coming from judgment and blame, which would leave the other person feeling the need to defend him/herself and unable to see themselves and the situation clearly with an open heart.

Another important point to remember when going within yourself to find the truth about a situation and yourself is that after you discover those things that you did or words that you said that did not coincide with being your best self or that brought a situation to a worse place instead of helping it, then it is time to take that understanding, learn from it and then let it go. Try not to go down a rabbit hole by getting lost in guilt and feeling bad about yourself. Do not kick yourself for too long. Be gentle and loving with yourself.

If it will make a situation better, it is never too late to remedy it with a sincere, open-hearted conversation using the new words that you would have said.

Remember, every situation can be changed when you change yourself to be different in it, because when you do that, you are shifting your energy and the result is that all of the energy around you shifts as well. If you are being your highest self, everything around you will shift to match that higher vibration. It is a universal law.

That is how you, being the love that you are, lift the world, and lifting the world into the frequency of love is a beautiful contribution that you can make.

13

DIVINE OVERSIGHT

The flow of the universe is a choreographed dance of movement of consciousness creating and expressing in divine, perfect timing with other creations and expressions of itself within a cohesive, interconnected matrix of light.

Consciousness expressed as, and through, a human body on Earth makes choices as the personality soul, while its higher soul self, or oversoul, oversees its human self from the higher worlds of All-That-Is, directing, guiding, shrinking or stretching time as necessary to bring its human personality soul into perfect alignment with where it needs to be, at the moment that it needs to be there to fulfill its plan. Or at least it does its best.

The job of an oversoul to try to be heard or felt by its human self in order to gently urge it into a direction or to remind it of who it is as soul or to jog a knowing that it holds within itself into conscious thought must not be an easy one considering that the human has the power to choose what thoughts will go through its head and what actions it will take in each moment, not to mention the random thoughts that are constantly flowing through a person's head that can impede the ability to identify a message from the oversoul.

Consciousness exists on many levels in seen and unseen realms, and it exists in many individuations of vibration and frequencies of light. Some light beings serve as overseers for humanity in a variety of ways of which humans are mostly ignorant and thereby are completely unaware of the intervention, assistance or direction provided to them.

Assistance from the overseers and your oversoul can manifest in a variety of ways, some seemingly magical in how they come about. Often they will send help in the form of other humans to intercede in a situation or event, human angels who will appear at the right moment with just the right skills and abilities necessary to bring about the perfect outcome that is in alignment with your soul's plan. Additionally, a human can be guided to you for the purpose of delivering a message that you may need to hear, or an overseeing light being may even appear to you to deliver the message itself.

These unseen helpers are not allowed by spiritual law to interfere with your free will, so when you desire their help for your own purposes, you must ask for it. They are always present and hearing your request at the instant your thought is sent out to them, but be prepared to experience that the answer to your request may not be in the form that you anticipate or desire. It will come about in the way that is good for all, in alignment with each soul's path and plan, including yours.

Something to remember when outlining to them what it is that you desire is to have in mind the bigger picture, the ultimate goal, leaving the details to them. Your oversoul, guides and helpers have a broader view of all of the intricacies of all of the connections of life, which allow them to design a much more beautiful, magical manifestation of your desires, more awe-inspiring than you could ever imagine.

PART TWO

MY LIFE
AS A SPARK

14

THE PLANNING OF A
NEW LIFE EXPERIENCE

You know your life as Angelina, and I know my life as Destiny, but how did they begin?

Each soul chooses their parents just as the parents agree to be chosen. As a soul, while you and your guides are planning your life, you are aware of the probabilities and possibilities of the life that you are going into based on your parents' chosen life experiences, their life circumstances, their personalities, etc. Of course, you do forget all of that information after you are born, which means that you do not remember that this is the life for which you have signed up.

Words carry a vibration, as do all things. If you listen carefully, or feel into it, you can discern a word's vibration, whether it is higher or lower in frequency, by how it feels to you and how it sounds. In that way a person's name, what a person is called, can play a role in influencing that person's vibration that they will carry through this life.

Often people feel uncomfortable with their given name,

that it does not fit them, and so some have it changed to a name that they feel better reflects them and who they are. I know that I chose my name for myself, not only for its high vibration, but to serve as a reminder for me of my life's purpose, which is to remember who I am as soul and to remind others of who they are.

I am sure that I continuously whispered *Destiny* into my mom's ear so that she would choose the correct name for me. Sometimes it works, sometimes it doesn't. My whispers and nudges almost did not work—After the wrong name had been entered on my birth certificate, it was later changed.

Before we are born it is decided by those at our planning table what circumstances and human attributes would be most beneficial for the desired life experiences. Often these are physical attributes, as well as mental and emotional, that are designed into the DNA, the makeup of the body and personality that is forming inside of the womb of its mother.

For instance, if a baby is born with a physical difference such as lacking an arm or a leg or maybe it is born with the anatomy of a female but with what might be the psychology of a male, these attributes will help to bring about inner and outer experiences that will lead to the growth of the soul and the fulfillment of that soul's plan. Yet prior to birth the soul knows its human body makeup as it is being created, as influenced by the mother and itself, and is free to choose not to enter and be born.

As soul I entered and was born into my female, human, baby body on October 22, 1957, and a week after recording my name as Dawn Joy McCune on my birth certificate, my

mom officially changed my name in the records
Ann McCune. My mother's explanation for
change was that I did not look like a Dawn Joy, ...natever
that name may look like. My explanation is that after all of
my intensive impressing upon her mind that my name
should be Destiny, she finally felt and heard my communi-
cations to her.

My skin was white and unblemished except for one spot
where there was (and is) an ink blot shaped, tan birthmark
that encircled and covered the protruding ulna bone on my
right wrist.

I read somewhere that birthmarks are physical body re-
minders of the places where, as a soul in a different life experience, that body had been injured or marred in some
way. There have been documented cases of people (a lot of
children) who have remembered living another life wherein they were injured at a particular spot on their body, and
in this lifetime they were born with marks on the same
spot.

That feels to me to be a plausible explanation, and if
such is the case, I am curious as to what injury happened
to my right wrist in a previous or future experience.

15

BEING IN HARMONY WITH THE TRUTH OF MY BEING

I did not enter my life as Destiny remembering all about who I am as soul, but I did know or remember or have a sense about certain things such as what was appropriate and not for living in harmony or alignment with the laws of Spirit and the importance of doing so. Though I did not know consciously what those spiritual laws were or even that spiritual laws existed or what might be defined as a spiritual law, somehow I just knew that there were ways of being that were right as the spark of love that I am that would naturally resonate with the order and flow of the universe, and I felt it within me. For instance, being loving was the right way to be. Being truthful (or being in integrity) and true to oneself were the right ways to be.

Underlying all manifestation is the unity and inclusiveness of the love of All-That-Is. In order to evolve in consciousness beyond the lower human mind, which is the purpose of our sojourn as All-That-Is in form, you need to know yourself as the essence of it. Then with that knowing, you learn to be it in all of your choices. You become the unity of it in all that you think. You become the inclusiveness of it in all that you do. You become the love of it in expression.

16

SHIFTING ENERGY

My sister Joy and I fought physically and verbally much of the time when we were growing up, and I suppose it was the result of the atmosphere in our home with a young mother who was struggling to raise four children, mostly on her own while our father was always either away serving in the Air Force or away because he and mom had been arguing again.

My fights with my sister were usually aggressively physical. I remember the day when after one of our altercations I said to myself, *I don't want to do this anymore. I don't like this. It doesn't feel good.*

It was a revelation to me, an "aha" moment. In that moment I realized that I had a choice in what I would participate in, and because physically abusing my sister and being abused by her did not feel like the right thing to do, I was not going to do it any longer. I became aware that even though I felt anger, I did not have to lose control of my emotions and fight with my sister.

As a result, the interesting discovery that I made was that when I refused to engage in an altercation, it naturally, automatically diffused the anger or desire within my sister to be a part of it as well. That learning showed me that I could shift the energy around me with my thoughts and feelings, essentially by being what I wanted to see outside of me in my world.

Later in life I expanded this knowledge of how to shift the world around me by using my intention to consciously "call in" the higher frequencies of golden white light and/or the pink light of love to surround a situation that I was witnessing in order to allow for it to be shifted into the highest good of all. Now and then I do the same energy work, as I call it, to allow the Earth and all of its inhabitants to lift into the highest light that is safely possible, always with the intention that it be for the good of the whole.

It is important to remember when doing such energy work that your intention be not for what *you* would believe to be the best outcome in any given situation, but instead it should always remain neutral to allow for the highest outcome for all. Only our individual souls know what the best is for themselves based on their plans for this existence and what they came here to experience.

17

BEING IN INTEGRITY

I am not sure how, but I managed to be true to myself growing up while at the same time following the rules—those of society and my mom. I knew what was right for me, and when my knowing and my actions did not coincide with what my mother thought was right, I am sure she felt that I was just being stubborn instead of what I was really doing, which was acting on the basis of knowing myself and my needs.

Because I had a sense of what was appropriate for me, I did not succumb to peer pressure. My desire to be liked by others did not overcome my desire to be in integrity.

One afternoon while sitting around a dining table at a friend's house with a group of other teenage girls, one of them dared the rest of us to smoke a cigarette. They all did; I did not. It was one of the many times that I put myself into an uncomfortable position for the sake of my integrity and doing what I knew to be the correct action for me to take.

That level of discomfort that I created for myself in the decision to not go along with joining everyone in a cigarette was nothing compared to the time when as an adult I found myself sitting in a chair next my sister Elise, her husband, and their teenage children at their Calvary Church. Elise had asked me to go with them to a function at her church, wording it such that my understanding was that I would not be participating in a service, but rather it would be just a gathering.

At this point in my life it had been quite a few years since I had left the Catholic Church at around 18 years old due to a conflict in beliefs, which created in me a feeling of being a hypocrite when I stood in church during mass reciting the required words at the appropriate moment that I did not feel or mean. By that time I had gone from being religious to being what I call myself now—spiritual—and I knew that I would never return to participating in a religious organization, because my beliefs did not coincide with theirs.

Thus, when I found myself sitting in Elise's church gradually realizing that there was a service happening up onstage that soon turned into a full-blown hallelujah, praise the Lord, accept Jesus as your savior, pastor's palm on the forehead, knock you backward onto the floor with the healing power of the Lord spectacle, I was not happy.

As the service continued on around me, in my mind I calmly went over and through my situation and the short list of options to deal with it. Knowing that I needed to do what was right for me, which meant that I was not going to be coerced into jumping up on that stage to be saved or even participate in the service in any way, I felt that I had two options—I could leave or I could stay and watch. I chose the latter option, fully aware that by making that choice to be noncompliant, I would be stared at and judged when I did not stand along with the congregation or reply when required.

In doing so, *I* became the spectacle that received the attention instead of the one onstage, and though it was most uncomfortable, I felt that I needed to be genuine.

18

FOLLOWING MY SOUL'S KNOWING

Other knowings that I brought with me into this life were: One, my sense of worth, which gave me the ability to maintain my love of self in a harsh, critical world that often beats down one's self esteem; and two, the truth that all of my answers were within me.

When I was very young my mother would say to me, as well as my siblings, "Don't you want to be somebody?" I knew that to Mom, being "somebody" meant having importance seen through someone else's eyes.

When asked that question, though I kept quiet, immediately the response in my head was, *I already* am *somebody*.

Other children went to their parents for advice when they had questions about life, but it never occurred to me to go to my parents or anyone else for input or answers to my life's questions or concerns. I intuitively knew that the answers were within me already and that they would come to me when I had the questions. The two go hand-in-hand, the question and an answer. If I needed to make a choice, I would weigh the options by determining what felt right to me using my inner senses. Though I did not know it at the time, I was following my soul's knowing that was guiding me and often keeping me on our chosen path for this life.

19

MY EARLY PERSONALITY
AND EXPRESSION

Growing up in the late 1950s and '60s was much different than in the decades that you have lived through from 2003 until now. It would be difficult for you to imagine the world that I knew, its slower pace, the intimate familiarity with one's family, neighbors and inner circle (sometimes too much familiarity) because they were the focus of our lives—that is until the introduction of black-and-white television broadened our view of the world a bit more by allowing us to see other people's real and made-up life stories and events.

There was not nearly as much content shown on TV as there is now, though, and there was certainly no Internet access or Web for browsing or social media sites, since there were not even personal computers, smartphones nor any devices for streaming.

As children living in a world minus those electronic devices, we rode bikes, played games, read books and created art, put together puzzles and developed our imaginations through our play.

My playmates were mostly my brother Dan and sister Joy, though there were also friends from the street on which we lived who joined us as well. My sister Elise, being six years younger than I, was too young to play with us so, unfortunately, she never knew the camaraderie that the three of her siblings shared.

I call myself a *nature girl*, having realized over the years how essential connecting to and interacting with the Earth is to my personal development and well being. I am nurtured by its beauty. For that reason, when I travel I prefer to choose places where I am able to hike, preferably through mountains and forests, forests lush with pine trees being my favorite spots. There is something ethereal in the sound of the wind that moves through a forest of pine trees, as if the trees are whispering to those passing by them.

I not only played outdoors, but I observed it. I admired the flowers and studied the grasshoppers that popped up from their hiding places as I walked through the dry grass in an open field. I noticed the seeds that fell to the ground from flowering plants, felt the thick, white, sticky fluid that emerged from where I plucked the honeysuckle flowers, and through the glass of my bedroom window I watched with fascination the bright, lime green tree frogs crawl and hop from branch to branch within the overgrown gardenia bush.

I caught lizards and stroked their bellies while they laid in my hand to encourage them to be relaxed and inert before letting them go free. In a pond near our house, just for the fun of it, Dan and Joy and I scooped up tadpoles in glass jars, watched them up close for a while, then released them back into the water, since we had no desire to raise tadpoles into frogs.

Climbing trees was also a favorite pastime of mine. In the backyard of one house in which we lived when I was in junior high school, grew a tall, mature pine tree with many thick branches that I would climb as high as I could, find a comfortable one to sit upon and commune with nature, with Spirit, with whomever was listening or watching from the unseen realms, until I could no longer feel my legs, because they had fallen asleep.

Barbies were introduced in 1959, and all little girls wanted to have one, including Joy and I. When one of us wanted to "play Barbies," she would beg the other to play with her, and if the other acquiesced, we would set up what would become our Barbie houses and cars as well as clothes and Barbie accessories on the floor of our bedroom, creating an imaginary Barbie neighborhood.

The pink, rectangular, plastic case that stored Barbie and her clothes became her home when opened and propped up sideways on the floor. One of each of my sister's and my faux fur-lined, booted pink slippers became Barbie cars, which they fit into perfectly as we pushed them around the carpet to drive them to their destinations.

I'd like to say we played happily for hours there on the floor in our imaginary Barbie world, but no. Inevitably, within a short time an argument would start about something, and that would be the end of that.

20

NATIVE MEMORIES

As a young girl I had what I would now call a spiritual experience wherein as I played under the giant willow tree in my family's backyard, through my feeling nature I was transported to what felt like a memory of myself repeating the same actions then that I had performed numerous times before as a different self in a different life.

It began with me picking up and holding a small twig, which had once been a live branch from the willow tree that I played near and that encircled me from above. There were several of these small, dried sticks on the ground around the base of the tree trunk where I squatted, and I found myself gathering them up to construct a pretend fire pit. I say *found myself* because it was as if I was subconsciously following a familiar pattern of action not consciously decided on by me, the little girl.

Once the miniature fire pit had been built by stacking the twigs in a crisscross pattern, my attention shifted to the ground, to the dirt, where I began to dig with a twig. As I dug, I discovered clumps of clay, which I instinctively proceeded to unearth and collect into a larger clump. Without thought, my fingers began to shape the clay into a miniature pot that, when completed, I placed on the fire pit where an imaginary fire cooked food within it.

Not even with Play-Doh had I previously shaped and formed a pot nor had I built a fire pit, yet as I worked on it, it felt very natural for me to be doing so.

Within my memory of this experience, as amazing as it seems to me now, as I was pretending, I was feeling myself as a native woman much older than myself who was reenacting a scene from one of my existences, this time as a native woman somewhere. Because of my emotional connection to Native Americans now, and since I have within me the DNA of Central and South American native peoples, I believe that America is the *somewhere*.

21

YOUNG HUMANS
AT PLAY AND REST

G rowing up, Joy and I shared a bedroom in every house in which we lived, each of our twin beds usually side-by-side, headboards flush against the same wall with a few feet in between them.

Though she and I spent much of our time arguing and physically beating up on one another, we were best friends and we were each other's go-to person of choice to spend time with in play.

At bedtime, instead of sleeping, we ended many nights exhausting ourselves while having fun together by quietly singing songs under our breath and playing silly, made-up thinking games as well as engaging in full-on physical body activities that she and I devised, which we called The Flying Nun and Mattress.

"The Flying Nun" was a favorite TV show of ours at the time about a nun who could fly when the wind caught her large headpiece and lifted her into the air. Our Flying Nun game involved one of us, with the use of both feet, lifting the other's outstretched body into the air over our own while we clasped hands, which gave the appearance and feel of flying like the Flying Nun.

Our other game, Mattress, involved one of us playing at being a mattress—laying still and not moving no matter what—while the other laid on and squirmed around on top of the mattress-body with the goal of causing the mattress-body to move, thereby losing the game.

Those nights we laughed hysterically while trying to be quiet so as not to get into trouble, which we were not very good at, and though we often got yelled at, we still kept at it until finally wearing ourselves out. The night would end with us each tucked into our beds, wishing each other, "Goodnight," and holding hands over the space between our beds as we fell asleep.

22

LESSONS IN
LOVE OF SELF

As a young child, and even through my adult years of 18 or 19, I was extremely shy. All anyone had to do was look at me, and a blotchy, red blush, accompanied by a heat, would start from my chest and move its way up to cover my face. I lacked a self-confidence in my beingness in the world, and therefore, I was afraid to speak—not only afraid to speak, but I did not know what to say. I had not yet found my voice.

A sufficient vocabulary was not the issue, because my mom has reiterated the story to me numerous times that since I could talk, I would repeat words that I heard, even though I did not know their meanings and though they contained many syllables and, therefore, should have been beyond my ability to pronounce. I also would repeat idioms, sayings or adages from memory with accuracy.

Upon reflection, I understand now what I wanted to experience as a soul with the personality of a shy girl who, though she could not easily speak up and share her thoughts with others, was born to communicate. In order to fulfill her destiny of using words through her voice and in her writings, she needed to meet the challenge of becoming confident in her knowing of herself, her capabilities and of what her heart wanted to express.

Singing was another one of my strengths and loves, beginning at a very early age, wherein I easily memorized lyrics and songs. I would make up tunes and add words to the melodies, allowing them to come out of my mouth as they would, based on what I was feeling in the moment.

One night as a young girl I remember feeling particularly sad, which compelled me to take myself outside to the farthest corner of the backyard where I sat on a cement block looking up at the stars. I was comfortable and comforted there under the night sky. Without thinking, I sang out loud to the stars the words that I was feeling as they twinkled back at me in response.

I was a member of the school choir at all of the schools that I attended from elementary through high school, singing the soprano parts of each song. I did not know how "good" my singing voice was, or not, but even if beautiful tones had been coming from my mouth when I sang, I was extremely shy and lacking in the confidence to perform and be heard. As one of many in a choir, though, I was able to blend in and go unnoticed.

In ninth grade I was a member of the school singing group called, The Triple Trio, which consisted of nine girls who had been selected out of the main choir. From within that group I was chosen to learn and perform a solo of the first few lines from the song "Over the Rainbow," a song from the movie *The Wizard of Oz*. It was my very first solo— and my last. I practiced my part in the classroom and at home and felt confident in my ability to sing it in the up-coming performance for the community in the school auditorium.

My dad was going to be in the audience along with the rest of my family, which excited me, because I do not remember him ever attending any of my other performances. Being in the Air Force, he was either stationed somewhere too far away to come or perhaps he and my mom were in the midst of another separation.

At the start of the song I stepped forward into the spotlight to single myself out as the soloist. Naturally, I was nervous knowing that all eyes were on me, and, as happened whenever I was the center of attention, I felt my chest and face turn splotchy red. I did not know how nervous I was, though, until I opened my mouth to sing. All through the solo my voice shook uncontrollably, and I could barely finish my part. Of course, by the end I was mortified and embarrassed and ultimately disappointed that my dad was witness to the disaster.

Many of my life's experiences as Destiny were planned prior to my birth, the details to be decided by me through the choices that I would make along the way. They came to fruition in order to build my self-esteem, confidence and inner strength. These were some of the life lessons that I came to Earth to attain. That means that I needed to live through hardships and occurrences that would bring about opportunities for me to respond confidently, with my own sense of self and self-worth. As I grew in confidence, that would then allow me to know my value and unique voice, that piece that I came to offer to the world, and then have the strength to share it.

There is a gift of learning and self-awareness in every event that you see and experience.

These opportunities to learn these life lessons would continue to present themselves to me until I could respond to them each time from the love of myself, knowing who I am and appreciating who I am, without allowing anyone else's thoughts of me to be important or override my own feelings about myself. I also needed to learn when it was appropriate to speak and when not, and how to speak my truth with love, never intending to harm another or to diminish another's light with my judgments.

One of the hardships that I endured began in elementary school from an accident, and its ramifications that continued through 7th grade, that then shifted to a similar kind of hardship through high school. Remembering that I was already shy, the incident brought about circumstances that would want to make me even more introverted.

I believe that I have always been a balanced mix of feminine and masculine energy in my makeup. For example, I loved being graceful when dancing ballet and felt that sense of what it was to be feminine, but at the same time I considered myself to be a tomboy, wanting to be outdoors, running, exploring and climbing trees.

On a deeper level, the expression of the nature of masculine energy can be thought of as action or *doing* and feminine energy as *being*.

An activity in elementary school that exhilarated me was climbing and playing on the bars in the schoolyard. I could either be found there at recess or playing hopscotch, tetherball or foursquare, or even in the field playing marbles with other kids at one school in particular.

This story begins on my school playground in Novato, California where I was in fourth grade in my ninth year in this life. I can see proof that what happened there occurred in that time frame when I look at my school photographs, because it was the year that I stopped smiling.

I was having a great time playing by myself on the bars at lunchtime, swinging and propelling my body in circles around the horizontal bar. Later I walked over to the long bar which had small, evenly spaced rings that hung from it. At one end of the bar was a footstep about a foot and a half off of the ground, which was there for the purpose of raising one's body high enough to reach the rings.

After lifting my leg and placing my shoe onto the footstep, I hoisted my body up to reach for the nearest ring, which caused my foot to slip off of the step and my body to fling forward. My mouth hit the thick metal pole, breaking off a piece of my top right front tooth. The broken tooth did not expose the nerve, but I was left with a triangular-shaped tooth, something that I noticed with distress as I ran my tongue over it. I also realized that since the broken piece was not in my mouth, it had to be on the ground lost in the sand. The rest of the details of that afternoon are a blur in my memory, though, the trauma of it all being the likely reason.

The tooth needed a crown, and as a military family, our dentist was located on the Air Force base. I am unsure of the reason, but my chipped tooth was capped with a silver crown instead of one made of porcelain that would have matched the color of my other teeth. Whether it was because we did not have a lot of money to pay for a porcelain crown or because the military did not want to pay for it or maybe because the military did not offer porcelain crowns as an option, whatever the reason, I ended up with a shiny silver crown on my front tooth.

Thereafter, for the next few years at school, I was to be known as, and called by some insensitive kids, the name *Silver Tooth*, hence the reason I never smiled until, finally, the silver crown was replaced with a porcelain one. As circumstances would have it, though, in 10th grade my smile disappeared again after having much-needed silver braces installed onto my teeth.

They were to have been required for only two years, but to my disappointment it turned out to be all three years of high school. After a stressful period of time wondering whether they would come off before my graduation, they were removed just weeks before my senior photos were taken. Within those photos it can be seen that I was happily smiling again.

It is interesting to me how these circumstances in my life not only created the shy, insecure girl that I became, but they also would be the catalysts to assist me in regaining my confidence and self-esteem. You might think that it was a strange way of doing it—my soul choosing to put me into situations where I could further retreat inside of myself so that I could emerge this confident, smiling being—but with those experiences I learned many lessons.

Your greatest challenges can bring your greatest learnings, and through my challenges, and the realizations about myself and the world that came as a result of them, I was transformed into a new being with new perceptions.

For one, I learned that my self-esteem and self-worth are not tied to, or a reflection of, my outside appearance. Self-worth is about loving yourself, appreciating yourself for who you are inside as the Spark of All-That-Is and the person that you are.

Additionally, from these early experiences I came away with another new perception which was the understanding that what other people think about me is not important. Good or bad, positive or negative, it does not matter what others think of me. What truly matters is what I think and how I feel about myself, always remembering who I am as soul. When I remember that I am soul, I cannot help but feel that I am the power and the love of it.

23

VISITATION OF SPIRIT

Each of us is born retaining the memory of the unity of all and of the truth of our being as a Spark of All-That-Is, though most of the time that memory is buried in the subconscious. It is as we acclimate to our surroundings and come into mutual agreement of them with those around us through perception and as we are taught the ways of this world that we learn the idea of separation, and we come to believe that we are separate from each other, forgetting the truth of the unity or oneness that we are in our essence as a Spark of All-That-Is.

There are those, though, in fulfillment of the life plan of their soul, who retain their unity consciousness to varying degrees after birth, and they remain open to various natural inner gifts of Spirit such as clairvoyance (clear seeing), clairaudience (clear hearing), claircognizance (clear knowing) and clairsentience (clear feeling).

I am one who was born with an awareness of my inner

senses of feeling and knowing, though I did not recognize those senses for what they were early on. Consequently, they did not play a significant role in my life until later as I consciously recognized these senses for what they were, practiced them and learned to use them.

Though I have a vague, other-worldly memory of lying in my bed at night as a child watching geometric shapes moving through the air, or what I now identify as light codes, and unrecognizable images floating above me in the dark that I would watch as my thoughts drifted here and there, I did not usually see the higher vibrating worlds of Spirit. Likewise, my clairaudience was not generally attuned to the higher frequencies of Spirit, except for the time when as a young girl, lying in bed on my side, one ear against my pillow, I began to hear celestial, orchestral music.

Wondering where it was coming from, I lifted my head to hear it clearer, thinking it was coming from outside of me. In fact, no music was being played that early morning as the rest of my family slept, and had music been playing, it would not have been the beautiful, ethereal music that I was hearing.

I laid my head back down onto the pillow, still hearing the music of the angels as clearly as before, now realizing, astonishingly, that it was coming from inside of me. Not long after it started, it stopped as abruptly as it had begun, leaving me to wonder if I had really heard what I thought I had heard.

Celestial music in particular has not come through my inner hearing since that morning, but Spirit does like to communicate with me through music, since I am musically inclined. Often Spirit will place a song in my head, most often a significant line from a song, that it wants me to take notice of, as a message for me. The line, with its corresponding tune, will play over and over in my head until I acknowledge it and consciously receive the message that they are sending me.

Sometimes the message is just "I am here," and it is the song itself that reminds me of someone who is special to me who is now in the spirit world. Other times it is a lyrical message from my team of light, my guides, who want to encourage me to contemplate the idea or thought that has come to my attention through the song.

Signs and synchronicities are ways that Spirit communicates with all of us, and I continually ask for and expectantly wait to receive more, as a way to consciously know and follow my soul's path.

Having been raised practicing the Catholic religion, I naturally learned about Jesus, or at least about the Jesus that the religion taught. I have since come to know Jesus as the master teacher that he was, not only in that life, but in other lives that his soul has lived on Earth.

As a young girl I had an image of him in my mind that came directly from the statues and stained-glass windows at church, which were similar to the blue-and-white robed image of Jesus that stood within the framed picture that hung within every house in which we lived. In one house it had a place in the hallway outside of the bedroom that I shared with my sister. It was the same bedroom where one morning I had an encounter with this master teacher, Jesus.

It was early morning and the house was quiet as all were still asleep in their beds, including my sister Joy who slept in the bed adjacent to mine. I awoke and turned from my side onto my back while adjusting my eyes to the light of day, and there he was. Over the foot of my bed, slightly to the right, floated a three-foot, full-bodied, blue-and-white-robed spirit manifestation of Jesus, arms outstretched towards me, smiling lovingly down at me. He appeared to me with the same face and attire of the Jesus that I recognized from the picture hanging in the hallway.

Having never before seen an apparition, regardless that it was this benevolent, loving being of Jesus the Christ, it shocked and *scared the pants off of me*. Thinking that I was imagining what I was seeing, I closed my eyes tightly to test the validity of my vision upon opening them. He was still there, arms still outstretched and still smiling down at me.

Now, knowing that he really was there and that I was not imagining him, and knowing that if I tried to make my way to the bedroom door to run away that it would be necessary to pass close by him, which I was not about to do, I attempted once again to make him disappear by closing my eyes. This time when I opened them he was gone.

I suppose that he came to me just to let me know that he was with me and that he loved me, but since I reacted in fear instead of receiving his love, I am sure that he did not want to traumatize me any further and chose to disappear.

Still in shock and scared, I looked over at Joy to see if she had seen what I had, but found her sleeping. After quickly getting out of bed and dressing, I did not return to my bedroom the rest of the day for fear that I would see him again, and I did not speak a word to anyone of my experience, especially not to Joy. I did not want her to be afraid to be in our bedroom, fearful of seeing the apparition of Jesus.

24

CATHOLIC MEMORIES

I know that you are unfamiliar with the various religions of the world since you were not raised practicing a religion, nor did I raise your mother to conform to the dogma of a particular religion. By the time your mother and Uncle Adam were born, I had disassociated with the Catholic religion, the ways and teachings of which I had been indoctrinated into from my baptism.

Growing up in a military family meant that we did not stay in one place for long periods of time. Among the many elementary schools that I attended after each of our family relocations throughout Northern and Southern California were two Catholic schools, one wherein I completed second grade and another a partial year of fourth grade.

My fourth grade Report Card attests that in addition to be graded on effort and conduct, religion was the core subject on which we were being tested, to which I earned first a B+ and then an A for the partial school year. Apparently

I was memorizing the tenets of Catholicism very well.

As a family we attended mass fairly regularly on Sundays and always, as most practicing Catholics do, on Catholic religious holidays, where on such holidays the pews were packed with parishioners, and at the back of the church it was standing room only.

We must have arrived late to mass on a few of those holidays, because in my memory I can see us, and me in particular, restlessly standing at the back of the church with the rest of the overflow. Arriving late would not have been unusual—Mom was late for everything.

Catholic masses are lengthy in general and agonizingly lengthy for a child, whether sitting in a pew or standing at the back of the church. The only positive to standing was the closeness of the exit doors when mass ended.

In addition to learning the Catechism of the Catholic Church, I memorized the scripted lines of the mass and performed perfectly its choreography each Sunday. I knew and recited dutifully every word of every response, when required, and performed where appropriate the continual sitting, kneeling and standing. I not only knew it well, but as a teenager I grew to love the ritual of it.

Though I am no longer a member or participant in that play, to this day I still appreciate and am emotionally moved by that ritual. I feel its familiarity not only from this life, but from other existences that I have lived, the memories of which are buried in my subconscious.

As a teenager, I went on a Catholic weekend retreat with some friends. It was held at a Catholic seminary where young men went to study to become priests. The expansive grounds had been set up for the weekend to host the many people who would attend. There were a few makeshift restaurants, an outdoor stage for plays and entertainment, and rooms in which to sleep.

My girlfriends and I worked for our meals in the Mexican restaurant as waitresses, my first and only experience as a server. When we were not working, we watched the religious skits onstage or followed a group of seminarian boys who wandered the grounds playing guitars and singing spiritual songs. Many people, myself included, gathered around these boys and sang along with them. We also attended mass each day in the tiny chapel that always overflowed with worshippers.

The whole weekend was truly a wonderful, moving experience for me. Love was palpable that weekend, coming from everyone to everyone, coming from All-That-Is and flowing back to All-That-Is. Our hearts were soaring with the music, as music will do, and I could not get enough.

I had an especially moving experience in the chapel during a mass one evening. The chapel was full, as usual, and I was standing in the doorway listening to the singing. As I stood there, my heart filled with the love of All-That-Is, and in turn I felt love for each soul around me. I did not know it then, but I know now that what I was feeling was unconditional love. Tears filled my eyes at the glorious beauty and the joy of that love.

Years later as an adult, in a conversation with my dad about being a practicing Catholic, he shared with me his view that though he did not agree with all of the teachings of the Catholic church, he did not see a problem with participating in it. I had a different viewpoint on the subject, which first occurred to me around my eighteenth year. That was the time that I began to feel hypocritical about being a practicing Catholic, because I did not believe in and resonate with many of the teachings. Being a hypocrite did not align with who I wanted to be, so I made the conscious choice to leave the church and not associate with any religion at all.

My newly-awakening spiritual self told me that the truth of my being, that of being soul, could not be found in any religion. It must be reawakened within me. All-That-Is was not a deity outside of myself. All-That-Is was me, as me.

25

VISITATION 2

On May 16, 1982, the month after your mother celebrated her second year on Earth, my maternal grandmother's soul left her body and returned home to the spirit realms, what some call Heaven. Your Uncle Adam celebrated his first year on Earth the following month.

My Grandma Marian had endured a challenging life particularly in her early years when she lived with my mom and a mostly absentee husband, from whom she would be divorced when my mom was two or three years old. Her second husband, whom she married soon after her divorce, I knew to be a difficult, crotchety, old man who did not smile and certainly did not like having my siblings and me staying in his house and eating his food those summers that my mom would drive us from our home in Northern California to their home in Southern California.

As a young girl, my mom was often beaten by her step-father with a switch from a tree, and on a few occasions when my family came to visit my grandma, for some reason that only he knew, and though he was old and had emphysema, he would chase me around the outside of the house with a switch when no one else was home to witness or stop him.

Of course, he was unable to catch me, because I could outrun him. Each time that it happened I would circle around the perimeter of the house, run back in and lock myself in the bathroom until someone else would come home, making it safe for me to come out.

Grandma Marian's ancestry and heritage came from the Basque region of Spain. Those family members made their way to Mexico then up to Lower California, as it was called then. My grandma was born in Los Angeles, California, June 2, 1912, to a mother who was born in Sonora, Mexico, and a father who was born in Pomona, California, but also of Mexican descent. She grew up on a small farm, and later, when she was old enough to get a job, she worked as a picker in Los Angeles for many years.

Grandma learned to cook Mexican specialties from her mother, and most of my memories of Grandma are of her in her kitchen preparing food as I watched. Even my dreams of Grandma take place in her kitchen, still to this day. She taught me how to make her recipes for beef/pork tamales, beef tacos in fried corn tortillas, as well as her frequently requested chilaquiles that were a favorite at gatherings. It seemed to me that she loved to feed people, and I have inherited that love from her.

Grandma was also talented musically. She would dance the Charleston by herself to the music that played in her head or sit at her piano and play ragtime music. I remember the look of her hands and I can hear the sound of her fingernails clicking on the piano keys when she played. Her piano skills were self-taught, and she played by ear. What I have no memory of are conversations with her. What did we talk about, other than cooking? I had only been in this life for 24 years when she left hers two weeks before her 70th birthday.

I was still with your Papa Joseph at the time and very unhappy with that life, because our desired lifestyles were not a match and neither were our personalities. The obvious question then is why did I marry him? The answer is that I was still insecure and did not have the love for myself that I needed, so I made the mistake of looking outside of myself for that validation, thinking that I could get it from someone else—in this case Joseph, because he was the only one offering—and I said yes to his proposal.

And yet, we did not meet by accident or coincidence, as all "important" people in our lives are souls from our soul families who have agreed to come into our lives, and are often those whom we have known before. Once they arrive, then we have the individual freedom to choose what those relationships will look like, how they will become and evolve, or not become at all.

I had not been in this life very long, and I was preoccupied with my life when I lost my opportunity to have conversations with Grandma Marian. I had not asked her about her life and feelings and learnings, all of which I am now curious.

I can have talks with her now, and I do, but they are mostly one-sided. She is now my guardian angel, and I can sense her occasionally, especially when I focus on her, but otherwise she remains very quiet and in the background. When I have psychic readings, she shows up to let me know that she is with me, but always she is very quiet with not much to say. Though very special in its meaning to me, her only communication is the reiteration of her love for me.

Grandma had experienced a heart attack a week or two before her departure from the Earth, and then another final one came, and the golden cord that tied her soul self to her body was detached as she left her life as Marian behind and shifted her awareness to the spirit world, reentering it to begin a new journey.

When I heard the news of her transition, I felt the loss deeply. I was still in my own life in the early stages of remembering and opening to my spiritual awareness, so I knew that she was fine on the other side, but I was concerned that she had not been ready to leave. One night as I cried for my loss, I asked her for a sign to let me know that it was okay.

Months later, while asleep in my bed, I dreamed. I saw myself in Grandma's kitchen once again, watching her moving here and there around the room while preparing something at the stove. Suddenly, as if the dream was being interrupted, Grandma stopped all movement, turned her back to the stove and faced me. Her eyes held love and gentle understanding as her words reassured me. "It's okay," was all that she said. That said, the dream resumed, and Grandma went back to cooking at the stove.

I awoke realizing that she had given me my answer in exactly the same words that I had used in my question to her.

I would have been happy with a longer message from Grandma, but even in my dream, in speaking her two-word response, she was her usual quiet self.

26

SENSING THE ARTIST

Painting was an activity that I loved to do as a child and still find enjoyable to this day, though I do not paint now. Time did not exist while I was immersed in the act of creating an image on a canvas, albeit an image that already had been outlined on the canvas before I began. I followed the directions and added the color to these pre-designed paint-by-number drawings, so really there was not much creativity involved.

There was one day as a young adult living on my own in my first apartment when I felt inspired to spend the day painting. I already had an oil paint kit that I had purchased long before but never had started. On a table I laid out the paints and paintbrushes, set out the turpentine and a rag, placed the canvas on an easel, and created a mood by lighting candles and playing my favorite ballet album, *The Seasons*. It was a beautiful few hours lost in the joy of painting enhanced by the classical music in the background.

As I painted, I became aware of what felt like a distant memory within me, a sense that I had worked with oil paint and turpentine before in another time and place. Their scents were so familiar, and I loved them, as much as I loved the act of applying paint to canvas to create a scene.

I never finished that piece of artwork, and in fact never really painted again, unless you count the times that you and I painted our watercolor Tinkerbells and fairies when you were little. Why didn't I finish, and why, since I love painting so much, didn't I ever paint again?

The answer to that question is that I felt that if I was going to paint at all, I needed to be great at it, most likely because I had been an artist before in another existence, but I was not good enough in this lifetime to be a master painter, because I did not have the ability or training necessary. In my mind, for me to be a great painter it must be a lifelong pursuit, which was not going to be my path in this life, so I decided, without consciously knowing it, that since I would never be satisfied with my level of proficiency, I did not need to pick up a paintbrush again.

I have a sense, from the bleed-through of that other life as a painter, that even then I pressured myself to be good enough to stand up to the great artists of the time.

I have had numerous psychic readings throughout my life, and the very first one came about at a psychic fair that took place once a month in a nearby city to where I lived. Your mom and Uncle Adam were very young, so it was in the early 1980s. In that reading I was told that I was either Mary Cassatt, an American-born Impressionist painter, or that I knew her and was close to her. In a separate reading by a different reader many years later I asked about my love of painting and was told that I had been a painter whose name started with the letters "M" and "C", and that I knew a well-known male artist very well in that life with whom I painted, that he and I were very, very close, and that I had some of the best times of my life with him.

Later, out of curiosity, I researched the life of Mary Cassatt, and I found that for many years she was very close to and painted with Edgar Degas, the French Impressionist painter and artist.

Did my soul experience a life as Mary Cassatt? Who knows? I do not have a feeling or memory one way or the other about the truth of that, but it is interesting to let my mind wander there through that possibility.

27

FOR THE
LOVE OF BOOKS

What you believe to be true will be true for you. I discovered that very important sentence in a book that came to me in an unusual way.

Like the majority of people, I was unconscious to the reality of who we really are and what being human truly means, and I was living my life in that way. I began on my spiritual path in this life consciously in the years of my twenties when your mother had been on Earth for approximately five years.

Since the first time I stepped into a library as a young girl, I have been enamored with books. I love the feel of them and the smell of them. I would find and "check out" as many at a time as I could up to the limit allowed, and after arriving home I would find a place where I could be alone, usually in my bedroom, where I could temporarily leave my life as Destiny and place myself in the stories that I read.

My favorite books as a child were *Susie and the Ballet Family* (I took ballet lessons like Susie), *Harriet the Spy* (I loved reading how she was the observer, watching everything and everyone and making notes about them in her little book), *The Shy Stegosaurus of Cricket Creek* (the story of a prehistoric dinosaur who interacts with a brother and sister), *The Wonderful Flight to the Mushroom Planet* (two boys who build a spaceship and travel to the Mushroom Planet where they meet the friendly aliens who inhabit it), and nonfiction books of butterflies and birds.

Later as an adult when I discovered metaphysical bookstores and all of the spiritual information available to me there, in my search for truth about myself and all of the inner workings of the universe and beyond, I felt that I had found my sanctuaries where I would return frequently to connect to my inner self for my renewal.

I am a researcher at heart, so I was doubly blessed in having so much information available to me. The key to using information though, as I have learned, is that information must be applied to your experiences in order to gain wisdom in and from life.

One of these information sanctuaries that I would frequent was the Alexandria II bookstore in Pasadena, California, the closest bookstore to where your mom, your Uncle Adam and I lived in Sierra Madre with my then boyfriend, Bernie. It was around 1988 when Bernie was kind enough to take us into his home, because I was not earning enough money as a new small business owner yet in order for us to be able to once again live on our own.

On one particular visit to Alexandria II Bernie was with me. I was happy just to be there, though I knew that I did not have the money to buy a book. At the front of the store was a round, three-tiered table that I made my way over to, which displayed the publications that had recently arrived. As I approached the table and began slowly perusing the titles, one of the books, seemingly from its own volition, dropped to the floor in front of me.

By the way that the books were arranged around the table, I was sure that it could not have fallen on its own. I picked up the book and read the title: *Attaining the Mastership*. After reading the dust jacket outside and in, I knew that that book was meant for me and that I had to have it. Acting in opposition to my character, that part of me that does not want to ask people for things, I approached Bernie, book in hand, and self-consciously inquired if he would buy it for me, which he gladly did.

I was aware that Spirit was acting on my behalf by knocking that book down in front of me to get my attention, to say, "Hey, this one's for you." Spirit will use a variety of methods to guide a soul on its path.

That book turned out to be a signed copy by the author, Elliot James, one of a small number of first-edition copies that according to the author were meant for specific readers who were ready for the information contained within.

Other editions were printed later with changes, though I am unsure what was different about them. Seemingly it was the wording that had been changed. Since everything is vibrating, and words hold a particular vibration, changing the original words used would change the vibration or energetics of the book, enabling it to resonate with either someone who is just beginning on their spiritual journey or one who is more advanced in their knowing.

To this day I consider *Attaining the Mastership* to be my *Bible* on my path to mastership as a spiritual being. Within its pages I was introduced to advanced studies to living the spiritual path, including the one truth that resonated with me the strongest, that what you believe to be true will be true for you.

What does that phrase mean? How does this work?

Your beliefs are your foundation from which you create your world. The creation of your experiences begin with the simple truths that you hold within as your foundation of truth. Therefore, each one's truth will be slightly different, unique to each individually. Where you see similarity is where your beliefs coincide with another's, where they coincide with your society's, or where they coincide with the world's.

Your truths did not originate at the beginning of this life experience—they are a culmination of beliefs that you have held in many of your incarnations. Before this expression of you in this life, it was decided which beliefs you would carry forth consciously to this lifetime in order to create a life wherein you would be able to experience that which would fulfill your plan for learning and growing as a being of light.

Nothing is forgotten from all of your incarnations. It all remains a part of you, embedded within your cells, within your DNA. This includes experiences, thoughts, feelings, learnings. All of these pieces of self are recorded, and many are utilized in each expression of you, of each existence, that which you can consider to be your underlying personality of the character that you have chosen to play in your life as Spirit in form.

What you hold within as your beliefs determines what is brought into your field through resonance with those beliefs, or in other words, what you draw to you through the

Law of Attraction. Possibilities are endless until the creative Source energy that you breathe into you is sent out from you with the vibrations of your beliefs, thoughts and emotions that will then be drawn to you and your life. Upon recognition of this truth, you are then able to consciously create experiences, or the quality of those experiences, by choosing your beliefs and thoughts.

If you do not like the output of creativity that you have manifested through thought, you may think again upon a new thought. You may change your beliefs, your habitual patterns of thought into consciously choosing what you think upon. This is the power of creation of your world. This is the power of you.

As you begin to allow for possibilities, what before your mind did not believe could be, you open the door for your beliefs to be altered, and a whole new world of experience will be available to you.

There were never many metaphysical bookstores in any of the places where I lived, but I sought them out after each relocation. Those of us who grew up in the '70s, and who were discovering ourselves and the world as young adults in the '80s, seemed to have a wealth of esoteric and spiritual knowledge available to us at that time in these specialized bookstores.

Books containing mystery school knowledge and teachings, ancient wisdom and philosophies such as *The Ancient Wisdom* and *The Master Key* were easily accessible and still in print. Through those texts I was introduced to the teachings of the Ascended Masters and others who offered information and answered many questions that I did not even know to ask. I was being led on an inner spiritual journey, an exploration and discovery of myself that is still unfolding for me today.

One part of my journey of discovery came about as a result of my friendship with the metaphysical bookstore owner of Alexandria II around 1992 when your mother was in elementary school. I was invited to join her in a study group with three or four others to learn about and discuss the origin of the universe.

The group was headed and taught by Marie Bauer Hall, the receiver of the illuminations and revelations of this mystical cosmogony. We met once a week in her home, the same home that she had shared with her late husband, the mystic, philosopher and author Manly P. Hall, best known for his writing of *The Secret Teachings of All Ages* and the founding in 1934 of The Philosophical Research Society in Los Angeles.

For me the early 1980s was the beginning of an accelerated time of expanded awareness into the truth of my being as well as the truth of the universe and beyond, where I was guided to places, people and information that were designed to expand my consciousness a piece at a time, incrementally, one piece leading to the understanding of the next.

28

BEING EARTH

Everything has a consciousness and there are different types. For instance, humans have an individual soul consciousness whereas animals are of a kind of group consciousness. The Earth, as well as all of her parts, including plants and rocks, have a consciousness.

And then there are those conscious beings that help keep the balance of Earth by caring for nature such as the elementals, the nature spirits, the fairies, etc., who exist in, and vibrate at, a higher density. The Earth and her inhabitants live in the third dimension, but simultaneously exist in higher dimensions as well that vibrate at rates unseen by third dimensional eyes.

Once, in the early days of my awakening to who I am as a spiritual being, when gathered with a small group of like-minded friends for an evening of spiritual camaraderie and meditation, we each sat on the living room floor of the apartment and individually set our intentions to merge with the Earth for the purpose of sending her light and healing.

In my mind I took myself into the center of the Earth, and soon after I felt myself merge with Earth's consciousness. I knew what she was feeling, because I felt what she was feeling. It was as if I became her as I merged with her. I was still conscious of me, though, because I also had my own thoughts while merged with Earth's consciousness. I was aware of being it, and I was surprised and in awe at what I was perceiving.

In an effort to experience more of being Earth, I shifted my awareness to pop my imaginary head out from underground to emerge above into a beautiful, lush forest. What I felt as Earth was love and her knowing that all was in harmony and divine perfection, which surprised me, because I had expected her to be in need of healing from humanity's debasement of her. As her, I felt no anger or judgment or any feeling of having been abused—there was only love for humanity and all that is a part of her.

From merging with the consciousness of Earth, I had a knowing that Earth is able to maintain her existence, to balance the imbalances, to do what is necessary to cleanse her energies, and she will continue to do so by shifting, through movements of her physical body land masses and oceans, through changing weather phenomena and even adjusting her electromagnetics.

The more imbalances humanity causes to Earth, the more shifts we will experience as Earth rebalances herself, which will directly affect our life here.

29

RIGHT WHERE I
WAS SUPPOSED TO BE

A series of events aligned and guided me to living the path of my soul, to be exactly where I was supposed to be (with a few sidetracks along the way) that resulted in opening my transcription business, and it all began way back in 6th grade when I wanted to, and did, take my first typing class.

Early on I was drawn to the creative arts such as baking, painting and sewing, and as I grew, I gradually focused less on painting and sewing and more on other activities which came naturally to me that similarly involved a talent in hand-eye-head coordination such as typing and tennis.

As kids my siblings and I were always strongly encouraged by Mom to take summer school classes so that we stayed busy. The summer prior to starting 6th grade, the two classes that I wanted to enroll in were sewing and typing. After enthusiastically presenting my two choices to my mom, she immediately tried to discourage me from taking the typing class.

When she explained to me that she had taken a typing class once and did not like it at all, in my mind I was aware that to her that meant that I was not going to like it either, which did not make any sense to me, because I knew that we were two different people. I could not be persuaded to change my mind about learning to type, so I enrolled in the class and was taught the techniques of typing on a manual typewriter, the only typewriter in use at the time. Every year thereafter I continued to choose typing as an elective class and gradually gained a proficiency in speed and accuracy.

Manual typewriters were replaced over the years with electric and then with computers using word processing software, and through it all I have continued to enjoy the challenge that has been presented to me of typing words on a page as fast and accurately as possible.

You come from a family of singers, beginning with my dad for sure, but there may have been others from older generations of which I am unaware. In addition to having a beautiful baritone singing voice, your great grandfather was a born communicator, which I believe I inherited from him (though I had to grow into it) as well as a decent soprano singing voice. From elementary school through high school I was a member of each school's choral groups. So was your Great Aunt Joy, your Great Aunt Elise and her three kids, as well as your mother.

I mention my musical background because it explains my choice of major when it came time to go to college. Being at a loss as to what direction I wanted to go in my life, because I did not feel a strong desire for one thing over another, and being under pressure in my senior year to make a choice immediately, I thought I would just major in music even though I knew that singing would never be my profession.

One thing to note about me is that I have never set long term goals for myself to attain in my life. I believe that I have always had a sense within that I would be guided on my path, which I have been. Perhaps intuitively I knew that the goal was not as important as the journey, the steps and resultant experiences and learnings along the way that get you and your soul to where you each want to be. Usually the closest I get to setting a goal is to make a plane and/or hotel reservation a few months in advance of a trip that I want to take.

The way that I allow myself to be guided is first to be open to the signs and synchronicities that are given to me. All of the guidance emerges from the moment, the place of now that I find myself in that is, therefore, pertaining to and relevant to that moment in order to choose the next step. I observe the moment that I am in and make a choice of which direction to move into next based on how each choice *feels* to me, feels in my body, feels in my heart. In other words, I am sensing the choices for what feels right for me in the moment. Each right-feeling choice then leads to the next as I take one figurative step at a time.

Looking back, I can see that I had been feeling my way through the early part of my life also, but without consciously being aware that I was doing so.

So there I was, a year and a half into college and still unsure of what direction I should take my life when a set of circumstances presented that nudged me toward and onto the path that my soul had chosen. It began when I was guided to read a magazine wherein I spotted a notice from a local, accredited college of business that was accepting applications for, among other courses, a 9-month executive secretarial course where upon graduation, due to their connections with local companies, they would provide a list of job opportunities for placement. After reading that, I *knew* that that was what I wanted to do, so when the semester was over, I quit college at the university and enrolled in the business college.

After graduating with the Academic Award from my class in December of 1977, I chose to interview for the job of the Personal Secretary to the President of the newly opened Film Security Office of the Motion Picture Association and was hired for the position in January, 1978. Located in Hollywood, California, the six-person office consisted of three ex-FBI agents and their secretaries whose jobs were to investigate film piracy and confiscate illegal VHS cassette tape copies of copyrighted films.

VHS cassette tapes and the machines to play and duplicate them were introduced in the U.S. in mid-1977. Along with this new technology and its ability to make copies of films came those who infringed on their copyrights by illegally mass producing them for sale.

Once again, without my knowing it, I had followed my guidance through their nudges to find myself in exactly the place that I had planned on being, and I know this because it was while working in this office that one day, through prior soul-to-soul agreement, a person very special to my journey stepped in.

Newly hired, 51-year-old, ex-FBI agent Robert Mann walked into the office, and into my life, unexpectedly but noticeably. It was not just his good looks that made me take notice; it was the physical, electric tingling sensation that vibrated all of the cells in my body as our souls energetically reconnected that lit me up, even from across the room. This man not only had a physical effect on my body in that moment, but he was to have a profound influence on how I saw myself.

As I have stated, I grew up very shy, and even in 1978 as a naïve, 20-year-old girl it was true. My voice was still in hiding, because *I* was still in hiding—unsure of myself and the world around me. Much was to change with Bob's help when, as I began to split my time working as his secretary also, we developed a friendship, a love, a relationship and he became my mentor. He helped me to see myself as the special person that he knew me to be, which gradually allowed a badly needed confidence to grow within me.

Much of our togetherness outside of the office was spent drinking coffee and talking at the local restaurant across the street or going out to dinner where we would hold hands across the table looking into each others' loving, adoring eyes, communicating the feelings that no words could, while the outside world disappeared from our view.

Though unspoken, Bob and I both knew that our relationship was never meant to be anything more than a short, deeply-felt reunion of two souls who reconnected in love, and about a year after he arrived at the Film Security Office, I quit my job there. I never saw or spoke to Bob again as we went on with our lives, mine including marrying your Papa Joseph a year later, and ten months after that giving birth to your mother, and fourteen months after that giving birth to your Uncle Adam.

One morning I had a vivid dream experience, or what in this case I call a visitation, because of its vividness that has stayed in my memory. The following details of that experience I recorded in my dream journal:

> *From where I stood just inside the entrance to a large building, I heard a familiar male voice outside calling to his son. Instantly I knew the voice to belong to Bob Mann, my ex-boss. But he had been more than that. He had been my mentor, my friend, my love.*
>
> *As I stepped outside through the double glass doors, he sensed my presence and looked directly at my face with joy lighting his. Soon we were hugging.*
>
> *"It's good to see you," he whispered into my ear as we held each other. "I've missed you."*
>
> *"I've missed you too."*
>
> *Time stood still while we embraced, neither of us wanting to let go.*
>
> *We walked hand-in-hand across the street to the Jolly Roger restaurant where years ago we would often escape from the office to share conversation over coffee and stare lovingly into each other's eyes. There we sat, together again, in appreciation and love, and drinking coffee.*

The warm feeling that I experienced from the visitation stayed with me as I left the dream world and opened my eyes. In my mind I reviewed each scene to ensure that the details would not be forgotten.

It had been eight years since we had spoken, and the more time that passed, the more guilty I felt at not keeping in touch, and the more I did not know what to say to him. After the dream visitation, though, I had a reason to call him, and I knew what to say.

Phone receiver in hand, and with a wildly beating heart, I dialed the number to the office, wondering which of my one-time coworkers would answer my call. I recognized Becky's voice immediately and reintroduced myself to her. After exchanging brief life histories, I asked to speak to Bob. She hesitated a moment before saying, "You didn't hear. Bob isn't here. He died of throat cancer three months ago last October."

I could not speak and listened in shock as she filled in the details and events of the last several months of his life.

Knowing that he had left the Earth brought a sadness that I had lost my chance to talk to him again but also an immense joy in the realization that I had meant so much to him and his life that he wanted to come to me one last time from the other side to say goodbye.

One important thing that Bob did for the office and for me was to introduce us to computers. It was the latest technology, still in its infancy that utilized the MS-DOS operating system which required programming. Bob taught himself how to program and run the computer and also taught me how to use MS-DOS, while continually reinforcing to me his belief that computers were the future and that I should learn how to use them.

Of course, he was right, and I did learn how to use them over the years as they evolved into personal computers that utilized the Windows operating system, teaching myself how to use each new software that I needed in my jobs and then later in my own word processing business. Computers have been integral to my life and making my living after manual typewriters and then electric typewriters were phased out and replaced by them.

Prior to starting my home-based word processing business, I had been working for seven years as the Executive Assistant to the President and Office Manager of a small corporation when I began receiving more inner guidance nudges, though I did not recognize them consciously as such at the time. As Spirit will do when it is time for a change, the rug that I had been comfortably standing on for a while was about to be pulled out from under me to make me take action in a new direction, and it would happen whether I was ready or not.

It was late 1986, and this time I had been led to a catalog from a nearby community center and within it a particular class that was listed among the variety of options. Only one title caught my interest—"Start Your Home-Based Word Processing Service," a class that was being given by a woman who had done the same for herself. I considered taking the class, but not seriously enough to sign up, and I set the catalog aside.

Unlike today, back in 1986 working from home was uncommon, but especially unheard of was providing computer-processed documents as an independent contractor for individuals or companies from home.

The idea of working from my home intrigued me as the single parent that I had become three years earlier, because your mother and uncle were 6 and 5 years of age at this time and in daycare after school that took all of my extra money after the bills were paid. I thought that if I could work from home, there would be no need for daycare and, therefore, more money would be available for the three of us to live. Though I was intrigued by the possibilities, I placed those thoughts at the back of my mind.

The catalyst that reopened the idea and desire within me to work for myself were events outside of my control that were occurring where I worked. My boss, the originator of the company, had decided to leave his role as President, move into the Chairman position and hire his replacement who would be my new boss.

It did not take me long to see and feel that the man that he hired lacked integrity, that he was led by his ego and that he had unspoken plans to replace me with a woman who had been his assistant previously. This man went so far as to start a file on me, kept in his desk, that he hoped would soon contain a document showing a growing list of mistakes that I had made that, I realized later, he thought would give him reasons to fire me. When I learned of the file, there was a single notation in it about how I had forgotten to include the attorney that we worked with downstairs in the lunch order that I had taken for the office that day.

My new boss was going to be the one to pull the rug out from under me and knock me down if I did not jump off of it myself by, in the least, making my work life miserable and, at the most, eventually firing me. I knew it was time to enroll in the class and open my own business, which I did in July of 1987.

Very often it is a good thing that you don't know what you don't know, but I was very confident in my abilities and sure of my decision. Most of my early years as an independent contractor were a struggle financially. I managed to gradually acquire clients, and as time passed I received them solely through word-of-mouth, but if I had known then how difficult life would be over all of those years, I am sure that I would have gone in a different direction and ended up still working for someone else in the business world.

What I know now, though, is that working for myself at home was part of my soul's path, all starting with that first typing class in 6th grade. Even when I tried to stray off of that course by taking a secretarial job in downtown Century City, California, in one of the high-rise buildings where no one saw or spoke to each other because they were locked away in their individual offices all day with the doors closed, after one month there I was guided back to working at home when I received phone calls from three potential clients. Spirit was telling me that all appearances aside, my soul's plan was for me to work at home for myself. It was what my soul wanted to experience, not despite the difficulties, but because of them.

In reviewing that plan over the last 34 years, I am able to know the reason behind it by what it has provided me and who it has enabled me to become. Having only myself to answer to, being free to choose how I would spend my time and having lots of alone time were for me as a soul the most important results of quitting my job and operating a business from home. There were qualities that needed to blossom within me that would have the best opportunity to do so under the circumstances that I was now within, which were all part of my soul's plan before arriving into this life.

Working for myself, having no long-term love relationship and little interaction with others allowed me the freedom to come and go as I wished, when I wished, to be independent in my thinking and choices, to decide my direction and focus singularly, with no input or influence from others. In the quiet of my many hours of aloneness while your mom and uncle were at school, I could recognize the free spirit that I am and explore my inner world of just being instead of focusing mainly on doing. I was allowed the chance to know and remember myself as soul and to expand into that in order to fulfill my purpose of being a catalyst for others to know themselves as soul.

As it was all unfolding at the time though, it was also a difficult life to live and accept or even understand why it was seemingly "happening to me" the way that it was. I would have much preferred the fairy tale life that I felt was promised to me from doing the right things and doing my best, and I felt betrayed. Always I wondered, *Where is my loving relationship? When will my life get easier? Where is my life of happily ever after?*

The answers to these questions could only come after living through those experiences. Only then would I be capable of knowing the insights, the gifts that I received from my experiences—these insights that I am sharing with you now.

30

HAPPINESS IS A CHOICE

I was not born a "sheep," not even a black sheep, as some might call me because of my unusual views, because sheep are known to follow one another blindly, and I have never followed others in any way.

We are all here for different reasons, to have experiences that are uniquely our own. Though they may be similar in circumstances and events, they are unique to each individual, because we are all of a different consciousness and personality, each of which influences how we perceive everything.

For example, many of us might be here to change the world in some way, but each way will be different, and one is not more important than the other. Some come into this world with the personality of an activist and feel the need to get involved in causes for change. Others, like me, are quietly in the background changing the world by shifting and lifting energy into higher frequency. We all have a part to play, because everything and everyone is a piece of this matrix of consciousness.

How to play that part, how to maintain that unique self while living amidst a world of divergent and diverse beings? You must be yourself always, doing what is right for you. No one else can know what is right for you and your soul's journey, though they might think so. You will be the only one to live it and live it on purpose, or in other words, consciously.

As I look back on my own life, how I have navigated this world of mostly sheep, who are blind to the world outside of the flock with its unconscious agreements of how to be, I see myself as I grew in awareness gradually feeling the need to be withdrawn from it. There is a well-known phrase that fits here: I was in this world but not of it. At the same time, I became the observer who was curious and fascinated by the sheep and what went on around me.

I have always been one who has required alone time, time to retreat from the energy of others and the dramas playing out around me to my place and focus of beingness within, where I could energetically regroup all of my senses. In that place of just being, away from all distractions, I am able to think and feel clearly, hear and feel my guidance, rejuvenate my energy and come to the truth of a situation or experience.

My early life was mostly a demonstration of experiences and examples of how not to be. Some people have positive role models throughout their life, as was the plan of each of those souls, but my soul's plan was different. My soul chose to learn through negative, non-life-affirming experiences, at least for the first half of it. My inspiration had to come from within me. And it did.

Throughout it all I never lost my hope for a better life,

nor the knowing that anything was possible, all while maintaining my sense of self and the sureness of the divine and perfect order of the universe. I knew that I was living the journey of my soul through, and along with, the intertwining soul journeys of others and the spiritual laws of the universe, but I also knew that I could bring about through those laws the creation of an uplifted life and self by choosing the appropriate aligning thoughts, feelings and actions that were infused with the frequency of love, not fear.

Along the way I learned that I can live that uplifted life and self no matter what is going on around me. It is okay to be happy no matter what—and it is easier to accomplish when I can release the judgment and expectation of how I think something should be and by not getting "wrapped up" in the drama around me. It is best to observe it thoughtfully, neutrally, from outside of it.

The realization that happiness is a choice came one day as I contemplated the circumstances of my life in that moment. They were the same circumstances that I had been in for many years, with only a brief year in between of some relief, after becoming self-employed with two children of 7 and 8 years of age that I had been raising and caring for on my own since they were 3 and 4. There was not enough money coming in to support us, and no matter how much more I made, the government took that much more in self-employment tax. To have additional income, I worked as a secretary for a variety of businesses on short-term assignments as a temp through an agency.

After filing my first few years of income tax as an independent contractor, I was struck by the inequities of tax legislation that would insist that a single mother of two be made to forfeit the earnings necessary to keep the cheapest available, yet still decent, roof over their heads and food on their shelves.

There were many days when I wondered what I was going to feed your mom and Uncle Adam, and over those years many tears were shed by me. Sadness sometimes enveloped me and often I questioned my guides and Spirit why life did not get better for us and whether I should be doing something else to make a living. I implored them to guide me, to show me my path.

There was one brief three-month period or so when my sadness slid into depression as my focus remained entrained and hooked into the cycle of thoughts of hopelessness and feelings of my own inadequacy. I credit my usually unwavering optimistic personality for finally returning me to myself, returning me to the acknowledgment of the truth of my being and, of course, also the loving guidance of the unseen beings whom I consistently asked for assistance.

Except for that few month period, throughout those years of financial struggle, I never lost hope that my circumstances would change for the better. I knew that they would. Most importantly, I learned through that experience, and one phone call in particular while within that experience, that happiness is a choice.

My "aha moment" arrived as a result of a phone call from a creditor wanting me to pay a past-due bill. She spoke to me in a tone of voice that was belittling, accusatory, threatening and insinuating that I was not wanting to pay my bill and, therefore, I was not of good character and integrity.

When I hung up the phone, I felt embarrassed at being in the financial position that I was in and then began to feel down about myself. But as I thought through the way that she had treated me and thought about me in relation to my situation, my sense of self burst through my thoughts to remind me that *I am not my circumstances* and *I would pay my bills on time if I could* and *I am doing the best I can, which is all that I can do* and *I don't need to feel bad about myself or be unhappy because of my circumstances* and, most importantly, *it's okay to be happy no matter what is going on around me.*

Just like that woman on the phone, society would have had me believe that the correct way to feel about myself and my life was disappointed and bad or even sorry for myself until my circumstances changed. That is the conditioning that we receive as we learn to navigate through life here on Earth in order to fit into society.

What I have come to know over time is that those struggles that I endured in the fulfillment of my soul's plan were for my growth and expansion. And though my humanness wants to apologize to your mom and uncle for having to endure those experiences with me, as a soul I know that it was part of their souls' paths as well for whatever growth they could obtain through them.

31

CHRIST CONSCIOUSNESS - ALL LOVE

Many years ago on one of my trips to the energetic vortex area of Sedona, Arizona, my friends and I decided to visit the Chapel of the Holy Cross while there.

Actually, it was my idea to go to the chapel. Prior to leaving on the trip I had been researching sacred sites in Sedona on the Web, and up popped information on the chapel. It is a site containing a vortex, or center of swirling energy that can affect consciousness and induce psychic phenomena, that is visited by many every year. As I read the information about it, I had a sense that we needed to go there for the benefit of someone in the group, though I was not sure whom. I was positive that we did not need to go there for me, because though I had been raised a Catholic, I had separated myself from the church and religion in general as a teenager.

We arrived at the entrance to the parking lot of the chapel in our car and drove up the long, paved road as it curved up and around to the parking area where we found an open spot. As we walked up to the chapel, I took in the beauty of the mountain that it is built into and upon and felt the high energy of the area.

The chapel is small, with a beautiful view of Sedona's acclaimed red rock landscape through the floor-to-ceiling window behind the altar. In the pews sat a dozen people or so, spread out, sitting quietly, listening to the softly-playing spiritual music emanating from the invisible speakers.

I had not planned on sitting in the chapel, or staying long at all for that matter, so I found a place to stand at the back where I leaned against a column. As I stood there listening to the music and lost in my thoughts, I suddenly felt a strong energy come into me from the top of my head that made my entire body vibrate. At the same time, I was overcome with emotion, with the feeling of love, and tears spilled from my eyes because of its intensity.

Feeling the need to sit, I found a seat at the back of the chapel where I spent some time experiencing what I intuitively knew to be Christ Consciousness, or unconditional love, that continued to wash over and through me. The love that I was experiencing was overwhelming. Not only did I feel it as me, but I felt it and saw it everywhere I looked. I was experiencing all of the life around me as this higher consciousness, and it was *all love*. Within that chapel I felt the love of the soul of each being, and I felt my love for them.

An elderly man entered the chapel pushing a woman in a wheelchair before him, a woman I felt to be his wife. He chose a pew at the front of the chapel where he parked the wheelchair with his wife still in it at the end of the pew and then sat himself down next to it. Before settling in, with no communication between them, I watched him reach over to gently, carefully adjust the sweater that draped over his wife's shoulders. It was a seemingly ordinary gesture, but I felt the intensity of his love behind it.

Eventually I left the chapel still feeling overwhelmed by what I had experienced within it and what I continued to experience while walking to the car.

And then I had to laugh to myself at the realization that I had been mistaken. It turned out that I needed to go to that chapel for *me* after all.

32

LEARNINGS
FROM INSTABILITY

The enormity of the totality of the truth and nature of All-That-Is and all of its aspects is unfathomable to our minds. At times when contemplating it, I allow my mind to go as far as it can take me into its infinite vastness, beyond time and space, and always the question arises within me, *So if all that exists is an offshoot or manifestation of this beingness or consciousness that is without form, whom I refer to as All-That-Is, how did this conscious beingness begin?*

It is too much for my mind to grasp, so my ego goes into protective mode telling me that I should be frightened of this idea that I am unable to understand, to which I lovingly thank my ego for its suggestion, then move past it to shift my mind and emotions back to this reality, the reality with which I am familiar, in order to regain my stability.

Life is filled with incidents that create feelings within of instability. There is a gift of learning about yourself that comes with each of these experiences where you have been thrown off balance or where your life has been turned upside down. They are opportunities to realize your own capabilities, strength and a newfound confidence in yourself, as you successfully go through these experiences and come out the other side unscathed and overall intact.

About a year before you were born into this life, my then husband, your Papa Rick, and I were invited to attend a wedding on the island of Maui. Six of the ladies from the tennis group of which I was a member would be there, and I had the idea to plan for us all a day out on a boat to swim with the dolphins.

In my Web search online, I found a dolphin tour operator, a native Hawaiian and his wife, whose dolphin swims were like spiritual journeys, because they included sacred Hawaiian prayer and teachings. I knew that I had been guided to them by Spirit.

The indigenous Hawaiian culture knows of the intricate connection and balance between Spirit, the Earth and us, and that we must protect and maintain that balance through our thoughts and actions, living in harmony with the Earth.

I realize now that my guides not only brought me to that website, but they also put into my head the idea of swimming in the ocean with the dolphins for the benefit of all involved. That plan should have struck me as being a crazy idea for me in particular since I do not swim, and I am not a fan of going into bodies of water in general, large or small, yet it did not.

I am not as drawn to water as many others are. Occasionally I will wade in an ocean or lake, but I do not really need to. Hiking mountain trails is where I prefer to spend much of my outdoor time.

When in elementary school, I took swimming lessons a few different times, along with my brother and sister. Eventually I could get myself from one place in the pool to another, but once I stopped swimming, I discovered that I sank. Though I had been taught how, for some reason I was unable to tread water.

My theories to this day to explain my inability to keep my head above water are that I do not have enough body fat to make me buoyant or that perhaps my bones are heavy. Maybe my theories, and I, are full of boloney, but whatever the reason, I still have trouble staying afloat no matter how desperately I flail my legs about. Something tells me that it has more to do with relaxing instead of panicking, though.

I was a member of the tennis team in junior high school, and one afternoon someone on the team had a birthday swim party in their backyard. Everyone was taking turns going down the slide into the pool, and it looked like fun, so I decided to join them. Silly me. The slide dropped me off in the middle of the pool, and I plunged down and then popped up. That is when I discovered that I could not touch my feet to the bottom of the pool, and I began to sink back down into the water.

I managed to get my head above water again, but I began to panic thinking that I was going to drown. Though I attempted to scream out for help, no words or sounds came forth to alert the others that I was in trouble. I sunk down into the water for a third time then managed to get myself up again thinking, *Doesn't anyone see that I'm drowning and that I need help?*

As I looked quickly around, I could see that no one was aware of me as I struggled to stay afloat—not the parents, not the kids. I knew that I was going to have to save myself, so I did. With a determination born of frustration, I made my way to the side of the pool and pulled myself up and out of the water while the partygoers continued talking and playing, oblivious to what had just happened, and almost happened.

Apparently I was so graceful at drowning that it went unrecognized as such.

Dolphins are a highly evolved race of beings originally from another place other than this planet, and the thought of swimming with them was exciting to me, something that I anticipated would be a spiritual experience. I was interestingly calm about the idea of swimming in the ocean off of Maui. I knew that I would be safe, protected by the dolphins, so I had no fear.

Before leaving the dock, the captain of the boat recited a Hawaiian prayer, a blessing to the Earth and us on our excursion, and also a call to the dolphins. We were given instructions not to approach the dolphins while in the water with them, but only to allow them to come to us if they wished. Then the ten of us were off, speeding out into the clear, blue water of the ocean to the spot where the captain knew the dolphins would be.

Minutes later we were joined on both sides and all around the boat by dozens of spinner dolphins who kept up with us, leaping and twirling in the air and playing with joy and abandon. They seemed as happy to be with us as we were to be with them.

I am unsure how far we were from the island of Maui where we dropped anchor, but I could see it in the distance, and it was close enough that the depth of the water was such that once in the ocean I could see through my goggles the sand-covered bottom where a few dolphins rested together, unmoving. Surrounding us at the top were the dolphins who had accompanied us to this spot.

I had only been snorkeling once previously in Cabo San Lucas, and then I had had a partner who held my hand throughout, knowing that I did not swim. This time, here in Hawaii, after inquiring from each of us our level of confidence and snorkeling ability in the ocean, and finding that I was not a swimmer, the captain chose to stay near me while in the water. Though I was not afraid, I was thankful and relieved to know that he would be with me.

Along with the snorkeling gear, solid-foam cylindrical noodles were supplied to keep one afloat if desired, which of course I desired. Being a novice in the use of a noodle, it took a bit of practice to balance myself with it wrapped around my back and under each arm so that I was not falling forwards or backwards. The most difficult part, though, was learning how to breathe using the snorkel mask so as not to fog it up or take in water through the gap between my lips and the mouthpiece that was created every time I smiled, because I could not stop smiling in joy at the dolphins that swam close by me.

As promised, the captain stayed nearby me and only strayed a few times when he dove to play with the dolphins who were close to the ocean floor. With my face buried in the water, my eyes followed him to observe. I was fascinated and in awe and delighted in watching him mimic the dolphins' agile, graceful movements as well as their speed, going in and out and around the dolphins as if he were one of them.

After a while, I lost track of time and was feeling quite content. At one point I placed my face in the water to look below and remained that way until gradually I lost all sense of myself and instead was focused on the expanse of the ocean and how peaceful the environment was. In that peacefulness I felt and contemplated how easy it would be to just let go of my body.

Then came the realization and feeling of the vastness of the ocean, that I was a tiny thing within that expanse, and I suddenly felt out of my element, that the immensity of the ocean was too big and not where I belonged. I began to panic, and I wanted to be back on the boat. In my panicked state, I stopped focusing on my breathing and started to take water into my mask.

Thankfully, the captain was close to me at that moment, and after dismissing my first instantaneous thought of how embarrassing it would be to reach for him in my panic, with an outward calm that I did not feel inwardly, I grabbed for his arm to steady myself, hoping that he did not notice how much I needed it, and held on with one hand while I emptied the water from my mask with the other.

I suppose he *did* notice, though—how could he not with my fingers digging into his arm—because to my relief, soon after, he let us know that it was time to get back into the boat and return to the dock where our journey had begun.

Thoughts trigger emotions, and sometimes, as in this case, your ego steps in to do its job of protecting itself and you. As in my previous story where I described how I sometimes contemplate the origins of the unknowable All-That-Is and how that triggers my ego to come forward to bring on a feeling of fear inside of me at the head-spinning enormity of what it cannot comprehend, when I was in the ocean feeling the vastness of it, my ego came forward again to bring on a feeling of fear when I began to feel uncomfortable in all of that water so that I would remove myself from the supposed danger. Yet in reality I was not in danger and there was nothing to fear, and I knew that, so I was able to talk myself down into a calmness after returning my ego to the backseat of my mind.

33

VISITATIONS 4 AND 5

My dad, your Great Grandpa Duane, developed dementia in the later years of his life. Our family witnessed the gradual disappearance of both his long term and short term memory and, therefore, the loss of his individual identity through the life he was living.

Born into his life on February 12, 1935 in Aurora, Illinois, he spent 75 years fulfilling his soul's plan, part of which was to meet your Great Grandmother Darlene. Together, in mutual agreement between all souls involved, they brought forth into this Earthly life experience four souls, my siblings and me.

Dad was in the Air Force and had lived 22 years of his life when I fully entered my newborn body in a hospital bed at George Air Force Base in Victorville, California.

Since as a family we did not relocate with him to all of the places that he was stationed, and also because of the difficulty that Mom and Dad had getting along with each other when they were together that caused them to choose to live and be apart much of my life, I hold only a few anecdotal memories of my life with Dad in those early years. Most of my memories of Dad come from visiting with him as an adult, often accompanied by your mother and Uncle Adam.

Dad had a loving, kind heart, though he could be impatient. He was a romantic who appreciated love songs and was a born communicator, with an announcer's speaking voice and baritone singing voice. In my mind I can still see Dad's face, his stance, his hand gestures, and hear his voice singing the songs from the musical theater production and film of "Camelot," one of his and my favorite soundtrack albums.

One highlight of his life, and a special memory that he held, was singing in his later years as an adult at Carnegie Hall in New York as a member of a choral group from his Northern California hometown that had been invited to perform. After many years as a member of this choir, he was unable to continue singing with them toward the end of his life after his dementia took his ability to memorize and retain the words to the songs that they would perform. It devastated him.

Dad enjoyed making people laugh and was the life of any party. In addition to a quick wit, he could express a serious side and liked to have intellectual conversations as well, of which he and I had many.

The last year or so of his life Dad was cared for in a nursing home. I had called and spoken to him a few times while he was there, both short exchanges, because each time he did not remember who I was to him.

Around 7:30 on the morning of July 28, 2010, having decided to make an apple pie to use the overabundance of ripe apples from the trees in my backyard, I began combining the ingredients for the pie's crust.

It was a typical high desert cool morning in New Mexico, so I opened the door to the backyard patio to allow in the air, which at the time did not have a screen door attached. If you recall, the kitchen, dining room and living room were laid out in an open floor plan, no walls separating any room.

As I worked on creating the apple pie, I received a phone call from my sister Elise who lived in Florida wanting to know if I had received a phone call from Dad's wife Carole that morning, which I had not. Elise explained to me that Carole had called her phone but she had been unable to answer it, and Carole had not left a message.

As we pondered together the possible reason for Carole's call, considering that Carole had never called either of us before, we both wondered whether she had reached out to let Elise know that Dad had left this Earth. When Elise and I concluded our conversation, I went back to making my pie, curious about whether Dad was now on the other side.

Suddenly and surprisingly a sparrow flew into the living room through the open backdoor and erratically criss-crossed the high ceiling of the three-room area, finally landing on the stationary ceiling fan. Not remaining there long, he immediately took flight, circling around and around until he found and perched on the rectangular smoke alarm box that protruded from the wall high above and perpendicular to the backdoor.

At this point I opened the front door to give the bird a second option to return from where he came, yet he remained in the house with me for over an hour, occasionally flying around, but always returning to rest atop the smoke alarm where he sat watching me make my pie. All the while I gently talked to the bird, telling him that he needed to fly out.

The sparrow stayed with me through the completion of the creation of the apple pie, and after placing the pie into the oven to bake, I decided it was time to enlist outside assistance to encourage the bird to free itself. I telepathically communicated, *Okay nature spirits, show him the way out*, and a few seconds later he gave me a look then gracefully, easily glided down and out of the backdoor, as if to show me that he could have chosen to leave any time that he desired.

As I closed the door behind him, a thought came to me. Knowing that spirits can come to us in a variety of forms, including animals, butterflies or whatever might grab our attention, I began to feel that my sister's and my suspicions had been correct—that Dad had left his body and was now in the world of Spirit, and that he had just come to visit me as a sparrow.

It was no surprise to me that Dad would be with me in spirit while I made an apple pie. Apple was his preferred pie flavor, but also we both had special memories of my visits with him in the fall wherever he lived, whether in Illinois or California, traveling to the local apple farm to pick our favorite McIntosh apples as well as to eat warm apple donuts and, of course, apple pie.

At 10:00 that morning I did receive a phone call from Carole informing me of Dad's passing the night before at 9:45. He had just had a shave by one of the caregivers, and then, after contentedly finishing his favorite strawberry yogurt drink, he laid back, closed his eyes, and peacefully left his body.

Within a month of Dad leaving his physical body, your mother, you, your Uncle Adam and his then wife, and I with Papa Rick flew to Maui, Hawaii, for our first-ever family trip, which had been planned many months in advance. You had celebrated your seventh birthday that year, and you were so excited to be traveling to Hawaii. Your mother and I knew how much you loved the ocean and how your heart would sing as you played in the water.

Your baby doll, Sarah, as I am sure you remember, accompanied us on the trip, wearing the new dress that I had made for her. Inside her green-and-white animal-covered diaper bag was packed the flowery, multicolored swimsuit that I had sewed for her to wear to the beach.

It was a wonderful trip filled with many firsts for all of us, such as snorkeling off the southwest coast of Maui among the colorful fish and large sea turtles, being entertained over dinner by Hawaiian music and hula, and being charged the exorbitant amount of $50 for one large Round Table pizza for dinner one night.

You may not remember the most amazing and joyful experience, though, that occurred in the condo which we had rented. After preparing a hot, cheesy appetizer dip to snack on before dinner, I carried it outside to the balcony where we all sat around the circular glass-topped table talking and digging potato chips into it.

Not long after we gathered outside, a Citrus Swallowtail butterfly joined us, alighting briefly on an empty cane chair at the table then fluttering to land on the top right corner of the screen door where it remained in our presence, unmoving from that spot.

We found it unusual that this butterfly had no desire to

be anywhere else but with us, and we wondered whether your Grandpa Duane, now in spirit form, had come to us as this swallowtail to make himself known, to say hello, to join the party and to assure us that all was well with him. Suspicion became belief when, after opening the screen door to reenter the condo, the butterfly flew in with us. Where we went, he followed.

His next chosen place to alight was on the sleeve of the t-shirt that your Uncle Adam was wearing. He seemed quite content there merging with Adam's energy for a time as Adam playfully engaged with him through hand movements, almost touching his wings, daring him to fly away in a game of chicken. True to form, once again Dad was the center of attention and the life of our party.

Having left the screen door open for Dad to leave when he desired, he finally decided it was time to make a move, yet apparently, because he was not quite ready to say goodbye, he fluttered back outside and attached himself once again to the screen door where he watched the goings-on inside for the rest of the night. Dad flew off before we awoke the next morning.

34

CHANNELING
AND MEDIUMSHIP

Two areas of study into our multidimensional nature that have always fascinated me are channeling and mediumship. I read books about how to channel, biographies of channelers and materials containing channeled information. For a few years I attended a psychic channeler's monthly gathering for channeled messages and teachings, and finally I took a channeling class to begin doing it myself. My intention was to open myself up to spiritual information from the higher realms that would benefit those receiving it, including me.

Channeling is a process that is natural to all of us. There are various forms and ways of channeling. You can channel love, you can channel creative inspiration, you can channel the wisdom of your higher soul or other beings of light from the other dimensions. It can emerge from you in any way that you express love or as artwork, dance, movement, ideas, inspiration, or even telepathic communication from an entity who exists in a different density, but essentially the process of channeling, broadly defined, would be the lifting of your frequency to allow a connection to Spirit in whatever forms it takes. You can channel your own higher mind or any other piece of the mind of All-That-Is. You can receive this knowledge as thoughts, as individual words, as energy, as feeling and/or as a knowing.

Mediumship is another metaphysical area that has grabbed and held my attention that I dove into researching early in my exploration of the self. Similarly as with the topic of channeling, I read what books I could find and attended gatherings where people in the audience listened to the medium give individual messages to a lucky few, messages from their loved ones on the other side of the veil that separates this world from theirs.

Through my investigations and personal experiences, I learned the importance of discernment when it comes to determining how "connected" a psychic, clairvoyant or medium is, or in other words, whether the information is truly coming from a higher vibrating source, whether the channel is a clear, open channel, or whether it is coming through heavily influenced from the filter of the channel's own ego self.

I discovered from an experience early in my life that someone may be psychic, clairvoyant, a medium or have other spiritual gifts, but it does not mean that they have done the inner work on their human selves to allow them to live through their heart-mind instead of identifying with the voice of their ego.

Mediumship is not something that I have practiced much in order to strengthen those spiritual "muscles," but after the soul of my sister Joy's common-law husband, Bob, left the Earth, I volunteered to tune into him to see if I could connect with him in order to receive a personal message for Joy.

Alone, in the quiet of my living room, sitting upright on the couch, I relaxed and lifted my frequency through meditation, envisioning Bob in my mind's eye, remembering the feel of his energy and personality, and I telepathically called out to him to request a message for my sister.

Of the variety of ways that we can receive insight from Spirit using intuitive channels, the ways that are more natural and easy for me are by seeing it as images in my mind, hearing it and feeling the knowing of it. That means that I am using clairvoyance (clear seeing), clairaudience (clear hearing) and clairsentience with claircognizance (clear feeling and clear knowing).

As I tuned in, all of these senses were activated as Bob came to me and connected his energy with my energy and impressed my mind with images and sound. On the inner screen of my mind what appeared first was an image of Bob and an airplane. Coming to me more clearly than the image was the sense or knowing that he was jumping out of a plane, which triggered the memory that Bob had been a paratrooper in the 101st Airborne during the Vietnam War.

Next I became aware of a song, and in particular a lyric from that song, playing in my head, repeating over and over—"Free Falling." I recognized the lyric and tune to be from Tom Petty's song titled *Free Fallin'*. As I listened to the melody and words, I felt that I was being given the message that, *I am flying now. I am free.* There were also other words and thoughts that I received from Bob that were personal messages for Joy.

As will often happen when receiving channeled or intuitive messages, your lower mind will balk and question
whether the information being received is really coming
from someone other than yourself or whether it is coming
from your own mind. Naturally, this is especially true when
you are familiar with the person whom you are contacting
in spirit through a personal association, as was the case
here. Bob and Joy had been together many years, and she
took care of him before he left this Earth as his body struggled with cancer.

I delivered Bob's message to my sister, though inside of
me I still wondered if I had truly seen and heard from him
or if it had been purely conjured from my imagination.

Perhaps a week later I received an excited phone call
from Joy. She was sitting in a restaurant across from her
girlfriend at a two-person table and parallel to them was a
man and a woman sitting at their two-person table. My
sister related to me that she and the man, whom she did
not know, were seated on the same sides of their respective
tables, an arm's length away from each other.

According to Joy, neither she nor her friend had ac-
knowledged or interacted with the couple next to them during the whole time that they were there until the man
picked up his phone, looked at it, chuckled and, for some
unexplainable reason, leaned over to Joy saying, "Look at
this."

He brought his phone close to her face to show her what
was streaming on it. As Joy focused her eyes, she realized
that she was watching the halftime show at the Super Bowl
and listening to Tom Petty in that moment singing his song
Free Fallin'.

Amazingly, through this stranger and these unusual circumstances, Bob came through to Joy personally to let her know that the message that he had given me was real. I was in awe.

Life-affirming joy followed the wonderment, as it does for me each time that I get to witness how magically Spirit works, how we co-create with it to bring about what is good for the whole, whether we are aware of it or not, and I was especially happy to have the confirmation from Bob that I had received his message clearly.

Since being given Bob's message, now each time that I hear *Free Fallin'*, I know that he has dropped in to say hello. Years later, when listening closely to the lyrics of that song coming from my car stereo, I picked up on a phrase that I had not previously noticed, which I heard in that moment as another message from Bob. He said: *I'm gonna free fall out into nothin'; Gonna leave this world for a while.*

35

FAIRY VISITS

Not long after hearing in a clairvoyant message given to me by a friend that one of the things that I have come to Earth to do is to build a bridge from the lower dimensional frequency of Earth to the higher realms of the worlds of fairies, angels, nature spirits, etc., I began to see evidence of the truth of it.

Before receiving the message, I had already planned a three-week trip to Glastonbury, England, a place that I had been to a few times before. This time, though, I would go to all of the nearby forests and woodlands with the intent to connect with the fairies, elves, sprites and all of the other nature spirits and elementals. Prior to leaving on the trip, I had compiled a list of places to explore.

Each area that I stepped into was lush with greenery and trees, flowers, ferns, moss and toadstools of different varieties—just the kinds of places one would expect to see nature spirits. I probably would have seen them in a tangibly recognizable form if my inner sight had been more open, but as it happened, I did see what I believe to be a sign from them that they were with me.

On a beautifully sunny day over the English countryside, my friend and local tour guide Ian and I got in the car and drove to the next wooded area on my list called Ebbor Gorge. The trail through Ebbor Gorge begins at the car park where it ascends gently upwards. At its highest point is an expansive view of the valley below before the trail then circles back to the car park.

Along the trail Ian and I stopped to rest side-by-side on two boulders which were adjacent to a row of tall, green bushes. I was enjoying the scenery while letting my mind wander when my attention was caught by a movement just above the bushes about seven feet from where I sat.

As I looked closer, I saw what appeared to be a thin, curling wisp of white smoke that floated up while continuing to slowly curl around itself until it dematerialized a few seconds later. I was not sure what I saw, but as I stared in the air where the wisp had been, another curling wisp appeared in its place. It, too, curled around itself as it slowly rose up, and then disappeared just as the first one had. I turned to Ian to share what I had just seen, but I did not have to, because his questioning expression revealed that he had seen them, too.

Immediately I thought of the fairies that I had asked to join us on our walk, and I was certain that, with the display that Ian and I had just witnessed, they were letting me know that they were with us. Just to be sure though, I walked over to where the smoke-like wisps had appeared and shook the branches of the bush to see if I could recreate them, which of course I could not.

A month or two after my return home from England I was working at my laptop in my office. As I listened to the audio file that I was transcribing, typing on the keyboard and concentrating on the words as they appeared on the screen, out of the corner of my eye just above and to the left of the screen I noticed some movement. I stopped typing and switched my focus to determine what was moving, and to my surprise and delight I saw what appeared to be a thin, white, slowly curling wisp of smoke that disappeared as it rose in the air.

The nature spirits had followed me home!

36

ENERGY HEALING

Once upon a time there was a nature spirit soul who came to Earth disguised as a cute, little human whom her parents named Alexandrea. Though she was in a human body, upon our first meeting I recognized and felt her light, fairy energy emanating strongly from it. As many of our lives here, hers had not been an easy one as she grew into adulthood and all throughout her adult life.

Alex and your Uncle Adam met as young adults, felt their souls' attractions, one to the other, and then came together in first a friendship and then a loving relationship that lasted for many years. The friendship endured beyond the end of the relationship, and Adam and I both remained in contact with Alex.

Beginning in her twenties and throughout the rest of her life, being ill with cancer, the treatments to eradicate it, the cycle of remissions with its return and the experimentation of new treatments for it, all played a major part in

Alex's life experience. She accepted it all with grace and optimism, continuing her education and moving towards the life that she had planned for herself.

After many years of her struggle, Adam asked me if I would do energy healing on Alex. She was going to be accompanying him on his move from Tennessee back to California, and my house would be one of their stops along the way.

Though most of my energy work prior to that time had been by way of using my inner vision and intention to direct light and color through the use of my mind, in the healing session with Alex I would be facilitating the flow of healing light through my hands to her body. In bodywork healing the facilitator is merely a conduit where the healing energy flows from Spirit through the facilitator to the recipient of the energy.

My spare bedroom served as the space for the healing session, using the bed for Alex to lie on. With Alex's permission, Adam stood in the room off to one side to observe quietly. After darkening the room to create a relaxing atmosphere, I envisioned golden white light filling the room to lift the frequency and to allow only those of love and light to enter. I silently called to healing angels, inviting them to send healing light through me to Alex to bring her what she needed, then placed my hands, palms down, a few inches above her at her head.

Though I did not see the energy as light, the increasing heat that was emanating from my palms let me know that the light was radiating through my hands to Alex. Gradually I moved myself and my hands down the length of her body, stopping in places where I felt guided to focus the energy. When I felt the heat from my hands dissipate, I knew that the session was at an end.

After Alex rested for a short time, the three of us shared our experiences of the session. While my experience had not seemed out of the ordinary to me, Adam had seen something that I had not. He had seen light emanating from my palms in all of the colors of a rainbow as my hands hovered over and moved down Alex's body. Being a nature spirit soul, Alex would naturally resonate with the colors of the rainbow, so how appropriate for Spirit to use those colors for her healing session.

The next stop along Adam and Alex's drive to California was Sedona, Arizona, where my friend, healer, clairvoyant Lina awaited their arrival. Lina and Alex had planned another healing session of their own.

Not so amazing, yet amazingly to me, being always awed by the magic of the ways of Spirit, Alex went into remission again and remained that way for some time. Then it was back to trying new chemical treatments.

Perhaps Alex's higher soul chose an earlier date to depart this Earth than originally planned or maybe this gentle, nature spirit soul never intended to stay long and just wanted a brief glimpse into what a human experience was all about, a not-so-easy human experience, but the soul that was Alex left its body after 32 years in this lifetime.

As humans we cannot change another soul's path or its will through healing modalities or otherwise, nor can we know what that path is. Therefore, we cannot know what is best for someone. The highest thing that we can do for others is to ask of Spirit that they be brought what they need in the fulfillment of their soul's path and that it be in alignment with the good of all.

37

BILOCATION

D on't ask me how, but apparently I can bilocate—or at least my spirit can. On two occasions I have been seen in my spirit body by one individual.

You know this person as Ian, my friend from England. Ian and I met when I was on one of my many spiritual journeys, this time with my girlfriend, Heidi, to Glastonbury, England. By a series of serendipitous circumstances, which I would say the whole trip itself flowed easily from planning to fruition through the harmony of serendipity, when Heidi and I needed to book a taxi from the Castle Cary train station to Glastonbury, we were referred to Ian's taxi service.

In England our train pulled into Castle Cary station where I borrowed a stranger's phone to inform Ian that we had arrived and that we could be found in the waiting area. It is a small station, so locating someone was not difficult, even though Ian had no clue what he was looking for in his two women passengers. I relaxed into a bench seat, exhausted from the lack of sleep while on the overnight flight, and I waited with Heidi. The events that happened next seemed ordinary enough as perceived through our physical senses, though the full extent of them Ian and I would only learn from each other later.

I became aware that Ian was coming up the walkway towards us when I heard him call out, "Destiny, Destiny, where is my Destiny?" I was sure those were the words that I heard, though Ian revealed to me much later, when he and I shared our individual remembrances of our meeting, that he had no recollection of saying them. If Ian had not said them aloud, then I must have heard them telepathically.

Ian may not have verbalized those words in that moment, but he did confess to me later that he did not know how he knew, but he "just knew" that he had known either Heidi or me from another lifetime. I did not have the same knowing about him when we met, but what opened up to me slowly, emerging from my subconscious, was the feeling that we had a soul connection and that our meeting was no accident.

I found myself watching him and being curious about who he was the next day after he donned his "tour man hat" and became our guide through the stone circles and sacred sites as well as a recently-reaped crop circle around the English countryside.

The three of us were together from early morning until after the light of day disappeared, and in that time he became familiar to me. Heidi began the tour seated in the front seat left of Ian who sat behind the steering wheel on the right side of his European car, and I chose the back where I was more comfortable. From the backseat the conversation was more difficult to hear, so it was a good excuse to sit back, relax and speak only when I wanted.

I do not recall exactly how, but Heidi and I ended up eventually switching places after one of our sightseeing stops, and as I took the seat across the center console from Ian, I felt a bit uncomfortable. I became acutely self-conscious, as if I knew that he was aware and curious about me as well, and I wondered, *How should I sit? Ankles crossed? How and where should I place my hands?* I settled on trading off between awkwardly positioning my hands in my lap to moving each hand to rest on the outside edges of my seat.

Towards the end of the tour, Ian made reference to the nice day that we had shared, to which I replied that it was he who had made it a beautiful day for us. Catching me by surprise, Ian gently placed his left hand on top of my right, where it had been resting on my seat, in a gesture of acknowledgment and thank-you, which became a gesture of affection as the minutes passed with his hand still in place over mine. Accompanying my feeling of embarrassment, two thoughts predominated all others: *When is he going to let go of my hand?* and *Is Heidi seeing this?*

Based on his expression of tenderness towards me, Ian must have been pretty sure by that time that I was the one with whom he had had the previous connection.

Months after my return home to New Mexico, Ian and I began a friendship through email where as it developed we discovered our soul connection and resonance as twin flames of the same soul. Our mutual knowing of this truth came through to both of us and was reinforced as truth by events occurring between us constantly such as telepathic communication and hitting the "send" button of unexpected emails that were written and sent to the other within seconds of each other. More significantly, we knew the truth through the recognition of our deep, unconditional, soul-to-soul love that never wavered, no matter the differences in cultural upbringing or the differences and difficulties we encountered between us.

My spirit body appeared twice to Ian while he was in his home in England and I in mine in New Mexico. Neither occurrence was I consciously trying to appear before him, nor was I thinking of him in those moments. I was not asleep or unconscious, but somehow my spirit body was in two places at one time.

From Ian's recollection of my first spirit visit to him, he described to me that he was in his bedroom sitting up in bed when he glanced over to the armchair across the room and saw me sitting in it. I did not speak or communicate; I just looked at him. It was a short stay, and then I disappeared.

On my second appearance I was more active, and our interaction lasted longer. Once again, Ian was in his bedroom lying on his back on his bed when he saw psychically a large hole or portal open up on the wall opposite him. As he watched, he saw me emerge through the other-worldly portal into his bedroom. Thinking that he was probably imagining the whole scene, he turned over onto his right side and closed his eyes.

His mind was made to challenge his idea of the illusory nature of what he had seen when he felt the bed move and the duvet shift slightly over him as I laid down close to him, his back facing me. Ian remained still, his sensory perceptions heightened. He first felt the warmth of my breath on the back of his neck, then the gentle touch of my hand on the flesh of his upper left arm.

Gradually Ian's focus drifted from the corporeal world, and my presence near him, into the dream world of Spirit as he fell asleep, perhaps to join me there.

38

DIVINE ORCHESTRATION

I have been the recipient of divine oversight and intervention throughout my life, some of which I was aware as the events were unfolding, others not until the completion of the event while in review of it, and still others I am sure I was completely unaware. It happens for each of us, though most are completely oblivious to it as often their attention is scattered in many directions. The surprise and amazement that I feel each time that it occurs is not in that it happened, but in how magically and perfectly that it unfolded.

Your now-moment attention is what can allow your notice of not only the physical external events as they are happening, but also of the metaphysical impetus and the reasons behind what is occurring and the realization that they are being orchestrated by Spirit, by your overseers and guides. Becoming aware of being in the moment of "now" is a learned process. It is about learning to focus your attention on what you perceive around you in each new moment instead of placing your focus on the past or the musings of the future.

On a drive through the city in which I lived, to a destination that I do not recall, I became aware of a subtle shift in my consciousness and the energy around me, which grabbed my attention. In hindsight, I recognize that the shift was the gentle nudge of my higher soul attempting to draw my focus to what would unfold. I knew that something was about to occur, and as a result, I took notice of my surroundings in a deeper way.

What played out before me as I slowly approached an intersection, that I observed both from me and from outside of me simultaneously, was a perfectly timed orchestration of three cars within the interplay of the yellow, red, green light changes of the traffic signals. One of the cars was mine.

Instantaneously, I received the knowing as I watched the other two cars approach the intersection from different directions, from the speed at which they approached and the timing of the traffic signal light changes, that the speed and placement of my car in that moment, which made them slow down or come to a stop, was the only reason that they did not crash into each other. As I drove through the intersection, I knew that I had been placed there at that exact moment to prevent a vehicle accident.

Another occurrence where I recognized through a shift in my consciousness the intervention of my oversoul or guides as it was happening, unfolded before my eyes as I walked to the baggage claim carousel at the Albuquerque airport to await my bag. I had returned to New Mexico after a trip to California and had hoped to get my bag quickly, take the short shuttle bus ride to my car and soon be relaxing at home, but my higher soul had a different plan.

Before approaching the carousel, I began to sense that something was going to happen regarding my bag. I was unsure what—whether it would be that my bag did not travel with me on my plane, or something else—but the feeling stayed with me.

Then, through a heightened awareness caused by my higher soul wanting to get my attention, I began to notice the unusual atmosphere I felt myself within that was setting into motion a preplanned choreography of the dance of everything around me that would result in the desired outcome of my higher soul.

The first step in the dance that alerted me was the change of carousel where the bags from my flight were supposed to have emerged. Prior to the announcement of the change, my fellow passengers and I had been waiting an unusually long time for our bags to come out onto the carousel where our flight number had been listed, which reinforced my suspicion that something was going to happen concerning my bag.

On the walk over to the correct carousel, I became aware of a feeling of apprehension slowly building inside of me along with the sense that there was something about to play out that I could not avoid. I felt each of my motions fulfilling an unconsciously prearranged destiny that was mine. In other words, I was within a situation that was destined for me, and I could not change it.

The carousel circled, already filled with luggage and still filling as I hastily approached it to find an open area among the people where I could stand and wait for my bag to approach me. The crowd was condensed, leaving only a small space around me close to the carousel where I stood trying to get a glimpse of my large, purple bag. The unwieldiness of my oversized bag added to my feeling of apprehension and caused an uneasiness about how I was going to lift my bag up and onto the floor without hitting a nearby person with it.

As I caught sight of my bag and watched it coming closer to me from my left, I attempted to warn the man to the left of me that I would be pulling out a large bag and that I did not want to hit him with it, to which he paid no attention and stood his ground. Consequently, when the bag did reach me, I was unable to stretch in front of the man to grab for it as early as I would have liked. Instead, the bag was on its way to passing by me as I grasped the handle.

The events that were set into motion by my higher soul came to a crashing conclusion when, as I grabbed the heavy bag by its handle swinging it up high into the air to the right of me, gravity took over from there, carrying it swiftly down where it collided with the outside of my right leg at the knee. The excruciating pain caused me to lose all strength and collapse onto the floor, my butt finding a resting place on top of the sandal-clad feet of a woman in a wheelchair.

Time sped back up then, returning the scene around me, and me in it, to its natural, third dimensional pace, bringing with it a consciousness adjustment into my lower human perspective. I was back to an Earthly focus, and immediately after coming to grips with what had just happened, and blind to those around me, I switched into problem-solving mode, assessing first the situation, and then what damage had been done—in other words, whether I could walk.

One compassionate, male voice somewhere to the left of me interrupted my thoughts to ask whether I could stand. I have to admit that in my frustration at the predicament I found myself in at that moment, I was not wanting to focus my attention on anything but myself, and I did not openly acknowledge him except to reply by trying to stand and test the stability of my leg with some of my body-weight.

Just as before, intense pain swept through my entire leg. A weak "Fuck" came out of my mouth, and I dropped to the floor where, without the pressure from my weight, my leg was pain-free.

I am not one to throw around cuss words, but there are appropriate moments when one will unintentionally slip out, leaving me feeling strangely satisfied. That was such a moment.

My higher soul had made provision for the presence of a solution to every obstacle that I would encounter in getting myself home when it allowed for this incident to occur. Each of my needs were met in the aftermath, and everything easily fell into place with very little effort on my part, starting with the human angel with the compassionate male voice who, after watching me fall back down to the floor, helped me up onto my good leg.

Still not making eye contact with him, I suggested to him that I hold onto his arm as I hopped on one leg over to the bench that was a short distance away, but instead he insisted on picking me up in his arms and carrying me to it. As I turned towards him to wrap my arms around his neck, I saw the face of a handsome, thirty-something angel in disguise casually dressed in t-shirt and shorts, whose light I could feel emanating out from his body.

His female travel companion was equally as beautiful and full of light, and they worked together as a team to gather my luggage, search for and bring me a wheelchair, lift and place me into it and then wheel me outside to wait for my ride.

The male human angel, Jason, expressed his wish to drive me wherever I wanted to go instead of leaving me to be picked up, but apologized that he and his companion were also being picked up. Several times Jason expressed his desire to do more for me, and I felt his frustration at being unable to do so in his present circumstances.

Before the two of them left to meet their ride, they made sure that I had found someone to come for me, and then we wished each other well. The last I saw of them they were passengers in a four-door pickup truck driving past me where I sat outside in my wheelchair, headed towards the airport exit, Jason's arm outstretched and waving to me from his open window.

My ride to the urgent care facility near my home came by way of one of my two girlfriends in New Mexico, the only one who was in town that day, and the same one who was going to be leaving the following day to move back to her birthplace in Austria. There was no one else to call for help, and though she was stressed and under pressure to complete the final items on her checklist for her move, she volunteered to be my third human angel.

The injuries that I came away with from my altercation with my big, purple bag were two small, minor fractures of the right tibia under the kneecap and pulled or torn muscles in both calves that I later discovered in rehab when I was unable to stand on tiptoe using my right foot. My body was too heavy for the torn calf muscles of my right leg to lift me. The fractured bone healed seamlessly and quickly without any intervention or cast after growing new bone around the breaks—this according to my orthopedist— and I was healed from all injury within four months.

My premonition had been correct—something *did* happen regarding my bag. Now I am sure that you are wondering why my higher soul wanted me to experience a bone fracture at the knee and injury to my calf muscles.

Sometimes we never know why things happen to us the way they do, or even why they happen at all, while we are still in the experience of our lives, and they will remain mysteries until we leave these bodies and return to the worlds of All-That-Is where all will be revealed through a life review.

In this case, though, I believe that I have a sense of why I had the experience of being injured around the areas of my knee, calves and ankles. The explanation encompasses a few different, but interrelated, topics that connect the physical side to its metaphysical counterparts.

Before I can explain a reason for the occurrence of the physical result of my fractured knee, I must describe the symbolic meaning of an injury or ailment that is in the area of the knee.

There are areas within the body, including the knees and ankles, that contain energetic circles of colored light known as chakras, that are associated with and affected by your mind, body, spirit and life. In particular, my understanding is that the burgundy-colored chakra at the knees is related to your mission and patterns, and the magenta-colored chakra at the ankles is related to your purpose, destiny and freedom. Therefore, one explanation of the reason for an injury or illness around the knees or ankles is that it would have something to do with your mission and patterns or your purpose, destiny and freedom, respectively.

There is also another layer to the explanation of this larger picture and that is in how physical ailments can originate. Your mind and emotions are very powerful creators, not only in ways that you would want to have manifest, but also in ways that you would not. You exist as a spiritual body, a mental body, an emotional body and a physical body all in one, and they all interact with and affect the others. Simply put, your mind and emotions can affect your physical body.

A negative emotion that you bury within you that you do not come to recognize, deal with and release but instead hold within your mental and emotional bodies, for instance anger, will eventually manifest as an ailment in your physical body.

When you have let go of your fears, such as those that manifest as anger, then they are not present to manifest as illness in your body. Illnesses that develop that are not karmically soul-chosen are your body's way of showing you that, however subtly and unrealized by you, you are fearful (the opposite of love-based) somewhere in your thoughts and emotions, and that that fear needs to be released in order for you to be healthy.

As your frequency is raised by releasing your fears, you are beyond the influence or effect of the typical third dimensional world reactions of your physical, mental and emotional bodies to lower vibrating stimuli. The more that you release your fears and are being the love that you are as soul by maintaining higher vibrating thoughts and beliefs, the higher your frequency lifts and the more you are outside of and immune to the lower frequencies of illnesses. Your body will naturally be healthy and maintain its balance.

Not only are there meanings behind where an ailment is located in your body, but even on which side of your body that it manifests. From what I understand, the left side of your body represents an issue from the past, your childhood or another life, and the right side of your body represents an issue in the present. The area of the knee in particular also represents moving forward—or not.

Putting all of this information together, along with my own knowing of the path that I came to Earth to take and where I was on that path at the time of the injury, what I sense about the reason for my injury is that it has to do with the fact that I was not moving forward in my mission. I feel that because of that, the energy of my knee chakra was blocked and it needed to be released, which the fractures enabled Spirit to do. Sometimes it takes a physical injury to occur in order to allow for energetic adjustments to be made within your body by your unseen helpers.

There is another more intricate and inconceivable example of divine synchronicity to share with you of how my overseers and guides helped to bring about my preplanned reconnection to a soulmate that I knew from different lifetimes. The orchestration of this eventual meeting began for me in 2015 with my higher soul impressing upon my thoughts that it would be nice to take another trip. Then the questions were, *Where would I like to go, and what would I like to do there?*

The *what would I like to do there* part of the question was easy to answer, since I almost always allow a lot of time for nature hikes and enjoying the local cuisine in my excursions to other places. Where I would go was the bigger question and one that I sought to answer through online research of places to hike. After some random searching, I narrowed down the focus of my query to two words—hiking tours— and up popped the website for Wilderness Scotland, which stood out to me over all others on the page.

I had been to Scotland once before as part of a group of tourists who watched the landscape and scenery go past from the windows of our tour bus, so since then I had been eager to return to Scotland to physically interact with it and experience it with my feet on the ground.

Scotland has held a lifelong draw for me. Not only do I feel a kinship to that culture through my ancestry in this lifetime, but I am aware of a soul connection to those Celtic lands from other lifetimes.

Investigation into the Wilderness Scotland website and what they had to offer informed me of the variety of small group tours available including walking and hiking tours with their corresponding dates and descriptions. I got very excited when I read the details of a hiking tour through the Scottish Highlands, and since excitement is an excellent indicator of a positive direction to take, I decided that that would be my choice. The next step was to choose one of the five tour dates that were scheduled for that year.

How I generally choose when to travel is that I feel into what feels right to me. In essence I am allowing all of the forms of Spirit, such as higher soul and guides, to give me a nudge through my feeling nature of what month would be a good time for me to be there and then what days. I like to work with them in that way to make their jobs eas- ier in bringing together the aspects and people that will create the adventure that my soul desires to experience.

Through the website I paid the deposit to reserve my place in the Cairngorms National Park & Royal Deeside seven-day excursion beginning on September 26, 2015, which set into motion the magical creation of the events to come.

Further planning of and research into my trip included the decision to arrive in Scotland two days prior to the tour to stay one night in the village of Roslin for an excursion to the famous, mystical site of Rosslyn Chapel, then take a taxi to the Edinburgh train station the following morning for a train ride into Inverness where the hiking tour would begin that day.

I selected a car-for-hire service and reserved my ride from the airport to my accommodation in Roslin beforehand as well as the taxi for the following day, then focused on the train schedule options where I chose a morning departure into Inverness and purchased my ticket online. Seat assignment was not an option on this train, which left me a little uneasy about how much open seating would be available.

I need not have been concerned, though, because the car that I boarded was empty except for two couples who were seated across a table from one another having a conversation. I chose a seat on the left side of the train directly across the walkway from the four strangers.

Having excellent hearing, it was difficult to tune out the voices of the two couples. They all were speaking in English, but based on the accents, I determined that one couple was probably from a Nordic country. To my amazement, the other couple, as I heard them say, lived in the United States, and specifically North Carolina, yet the female spoke with a

German accent. To my further amazement, this American/German couple explained to the other couple that the reason they were on this train to Inverness was because they were going to be meeting up with a group of people as part of a Wilderness Scotland tour to hike through the Highlands.

When I heard that, I knew that they were part of my group, and in my excitement I uncharacteristically was compelled to open my mouth to speak to them to say, "I'm going on the same Wilderness Scotland tour." After that, introductions were exchanged and we spent the four-hour ride to Inverness becoming acquainted.

All the while at the same time that we were getting to know each other I was having a conversation with myself about the synchronicity of this meeting, that it was divine timing and too coincidental for us to be on the same train, on the same day, in the same car, sitting across from one another and on the same hiking tour. Yet there are no coincidences, and, therefore, I knew that there was a meaning and reason behind it—*So what*, I wondered, *was the reason?*

That hiking tour through the Scottish Highlands with that small group of special people and the adventures and camaraderie that we shared, remains one of my favorite trips. The American/German couple, Kevin and Christa, and I developed a friendship, and we kept in touch over the next few years until, after a long illness, Christa left the Earth, leaving Kevin to begin a new life without the woman that he had shared his life and love with for almost five decades.

Nearly two years after that trip to Scotland, in a psychic reading that I received, I was told of a special, loving relationship that was coming into my life with a soulmate whom I have known and loved many times in other existences. That was the good news. The bad news, I was told, was that first I had promised (from the spirit world, presumably prior to my birth) to spend some time with a different man, an "interim man," in a relationship that "wouldn't take much time to deal with," as the clairvoyant reader put it. You can imagine how unexcited I was about that.

As forewarned, the following year I met and spent some time with the interim man. Though I would not contend that our relationship was one that had to be dealt with, it did not take us long to realize that we were better off being just friends.

Over the years since the trip to Scotland, I still occasionally wondered and questioned why I met Kevin and Christa. It was just too unbelievable how it happened for it to be coincidental and meaningless. My question was finally answered when Kevin, now single, approached me with the desire to see if we would be good together as more than friends.

After he and I began dating, it became clear to us that our magnetic connection, the blissful reuniting of our souls, was undeniably the continuation of an eternal love that has transcended time, just as the psychic reader had foreseen and described to me. Little did I know while sitting across from Kevin on the train to Inverness that Spirit was introducing me to my future partner.

39

I'VE GOT THIS

Somewhere deep within my being I feel the sense that I as soul chose to maneuver through this human life on my own, to figure it out myself as a typical human by not being born with, and therefore not having use of, psychic and spiritual abilities, rememberings or other tools that I have had the use of in other lifetimes or in the higher dimensions. I wanted to awaken myself to myself starting almost from scratch with only my limited human senses and a bit of knowingness of spiritual truth.

I have a vision of me communicating with complete confidence to those who were there to help me plan this life's journey that, "I've got this. I want to do this by myself, because I know I can."

By doing so, I gave myself the challenge of discovering for myself in this life, through a variety of means, that I am soul and what that means in terms of how I create in this life, what I allow through co-creation with others and how

I recognize and build a bridge to my divine self that is my higher, inner voice.

As I tune into my inner wisdom now, I have the knowing that this type of path that I intentionally chose to take, the path of forgetting the higher-consciousness being that I have known myself to be in other times and spaces with the corresponding tools and abilities that I once had, was for a particular purpose. The purpose was to create an energetic road for others to follow who were like me.

There are many ways to expand in consciousness, and one of the ways the universe enables it is by allowing the energetically-created path taken by one person to be open and accessible to another. Once one person has a thought or idea or takes action in their own way to come to a particular realization, it creates an energetic path for others to follow that was not there previously in exactly that way, thereby making it easier for those that follow to realize the possibility and find their way.

For example, because I entered this existence as a human as most humans do, with no awareness of my multidimensionality, and, therefore, being ignorant of the possibilities that exist as a result of that multidimensional nature, my path of how I learned it and what my consciousness expanded into is now open as a possible path for others to access and expand into for themselves. When one creates an energetic pathway to a shift in awareness through the living of it, it opens the possibility to others to do the same.

Many of the circumstances and events that I have encountered in my life have been the result of my prebirth plan to focus on and explore a life lesson of trust. My decision to do it by myself with very few tools is the reason that I have often felt alone and disconnected from Spirit, those on the other side who said yes to guiding me, which required me to learn to trust Spirit to bring me what I needed.

I do not consciously know what my soul's plan is, but I trust that I am always within it and where I need to be in each moment in order to fulfill it. Soul's plan is not my human mind plan for my life experiences—it is that which was chosen before entering this life and any changes or adjustments that have been made along the way through the living of my life.

I could have chosen an easier way of life, but I *do* enjoy a challenge, and my guides know that. Of course, they have always been watching over me, always ready to assist in my times of need.

I believe, in our combined wisdom, that we chose to embed into my DNA my love of a challenge to ensure the perpetuation of my lifelong I-can-do-it attitude while in this body to keep me optimistically moving forward no matter how difficult.

Was it wisdom? Did I really need so many challenges? Hmm . . . maybe the joke is on me.

PART III

THE SPARK
IN EARTHLY
EVOLUTION

40

ASCENSION IS
EVOLUTION

Somewhere along my journey a question was posed that caught my attention asked by a woman of her friend regarding the soul and ascension. She wanted to know, "Are we supposed to raise our frequency or is our frequency going to be raised by merging with the soul? Which is it?"

From my own experience, I would answer this question by saying that it is both.

Lifting yourself in frequency begins through the realization of who you are as soul, where you are then able to release the false, limiting beliefs about yourself that you have learned to accept as truth throughout your life that tell you that you are small, powerless, flawed, insignificant, unworthy or even unlovable. The truth of your being is that you are a Spark of All-That-Is, which at its essence is love.

You lifting in frequency is you lifting in consciousness or

awareness. When your consciousness vibrates at a higher frequency, you are able to access the wisdom of the higher dimensions because you come into harmony with them vibrationally.

One way to accomplish a lift in frequency is to get in touch with your higher soul self through meditation, which essentially is the process of refocusing your awareness inwardly which allows you to detach from your outer world. Your inner world is where you realize your center, your beingness where you are one with All-That-Is.

Doing the work of raising your own frequency allows for your higher soul to merge more of its consciousness, its light, within you as you, which is what it desires to do. Through this transformation, you are ascending into higher frequency, into expanded awareness, into higher consciousness.

As you go through this process of refinement, becoming the master of your thoughts and emotions, thereby allowing your higher self to be heard by you and be your influence and guide as it merges in consciousness with you, then through initiations and activations your body becomes lifted in frequency by your higher self. You are then holding or embodying more of its light.

Ascension is essentially the process by which your higher soul, which is of a higher frequency, merges and integrates more of itself into your human self after it has been prepared and uplifted enough in frequency and in consciousness to be able to hold and integrate this increased amount of light, frequency and consciousness. It happens gradually, because each individual personality is the one who must prepare itself and its body for this deeper connection by first realizing who it is truly as soul and connecting more deeply to it by refining the mental, emotional and physical bodies through higher thoughts, loving actions and care of the physical body as it lives its life. Through the process of ascension into, and integration as, the consciousness of your higher soul, your ego is transcended.

As this process of evolution unfolded for me, I gradually became aware that I was perceiving myself from two perspectives simultaneously, that of my lower personality self and that of my higher soul or what can be called my oversoul. It is a feeling and sense that I am outside of myself watching myself.

When a choice is presented to me in my life, I know instantly from both the perspective of me as the oversoul and me as the personality soul, what is the higher choice (that of love, love of self) and what would be the ego's choice (from fear). Then I get to make my decision from that dual-perspective awareness. Will I take the high road or the low road? I will admit that sometimes, even in my knowing that it is not going to end well for me, I still choose the path of the ego and end up kicking myself later.

Gradually, as my oversoul and my personality soul have merged more and more over time, I have found that the dual perspective has dissolved more into one where the oversoul is the main awareness that my life is perceived through, and I am living more through the mind of my heart instead of my ego.

In addition to the individual ascension process, at this time in the Earth's cycles, cycles which are constant and that are tied to its continuing evolution, there is a global, Earthly ascension that is occurring. The Earth herself is lifting in frequency.

In the words of Orion, the star being channeled by Betsy-Morgan Coffman in their book *Ascension: The Accelerated Path into the New Millennium*:

> *"Ascension is the lifting of energy. This is a process and a destiny of human beings, for this lifting of energy we call ascension is quite simply evolution."*

One of soul's plans that is universal to all of our paths is the evolution of humanity in consciousness. Soul incarnates as human in order to evolve it into being all that it is as soul through an awareness of itself as the living expression here on Earth of that love and light.

Consciousness comes in many Earthly manifestations, be they plant, mineral or animal, for instance, giving each its own form of life, but as is the way of all consciousness, it evolves. The natural process of evolution of these manifestations of life are at this time on the accelerated path of ascension into higher consciousness along with the Earth.

Among the variety of ancient teachings that I have come across was a description of the process of evolution of plant consciousness into the next higher level of mineral consciousness evolving then into the even higher level of animal consciousness.

I encountered evidence of such transformation of plant into mineral on a visit to Petrified Forest National Park in northeastern Arizona. What once was part of the stump of a tree was now a remnant of a piece of petrified wood that had turned almost entirely into many facets of a beautiful, light blue, quartz crystal that sparkled in the bright sun. Its consciousness was slowly evolving into a higher awareness.

41

THIS HUMAN ADVENTURE

As we go about our Earthly lives, we must know and remember and get comfortable with the fact that everything is not as it appears to be and that there is much more behind the scenes of the workings of our world, and beyond our world, than we realize.

Be open to the mystery and the magic and wonderment of discovering what it is to be human and the truth of the history of the Earth and the universe. Have fun, play while you explore, and have a sense of humor about it all.

Try not to take life so seriously, because once you do and you get caught up in the drama, then you are living in and can become stuck in the lower frequencies of the illusion of this game that we are playing, this game of coming to Earth with temporary amnesia so as to believe in the illusion that you are only a human in the third dimension and nothing more.

Cultivate joy. Sow it, feed it by being in joy, by doing

what makes you feel lifted and happy. When you are sending out that feeling and accelerated frequency of joyfulness, as with all types of frequency that you emit, you are drawing to you more of the same.

Life on Earth was not meant to be easy, but it can be a great adventure if you are ready to experience it in that way. Each of us forgot, after leaving the unlimited bliss of the spirit worlds and arriving here, that we came for the express purpose of delving deep into the messiness of life as a human on Earth and to participate in its evolution. We were offered the opportunity to experience and evolve as a human using all of our human senses in any way that we would choose, senses that are not available to us in the same way in the world of Spirit, and we all enthusiastically and eagerly said, "Yes, count me in."

Be gentle and loving with yourself as you make what you consider to be mistakes, as you grow in awareness through experience. Be kind, understanding and forgiving of others as they make their mistakes. We are all just trying to make our way in the world the best that we know how, often oblivious to how we hurt each other.

I have been blessed to be in this adventure with you, my Angelina, and all of those souls who wanted to take this ride with me. Thanks for being a part of my life.

NOTES

CHAPTER 3

p. 27: *The Complete Ascension Manual: How to Achieve Ascension in this Lifetime* by Joshua David Stone, Ph.D., copyright © 1994 by Joshua David Stone, published by Light Technology Publishing. Used by permission of Light Technology Publishing.

CHAPTER 40

p. 186: *Ascension: The Accelerated Path into the New Millennium* by Betsy-Morgan Coffman, copyright © 2009 by Betsy-Morgan Coffman, published by Gabriel Light Publishing. Used by permission of Gabriel Light Publishing.

CPSIA information can be obtained
at www.ICGtesting.com
Printed in the USA
LVHW031613240323
742408LV00004B/877

9 781737 917403